T0083977

G

Gallery Books

New York

London

Toronto

Sydney

New Delhi

SELP-HELF

by
Miranda
Sings

G

Gallery Books
An Imprint of Simon & Schuster, Inc.
1230 Avenue of the Americas
New York, NY 10020

Copyright © 2015 by Miranda Sings, Inc.

All rights reserved, including the right to reproduce this book or portions thereof in any form whatsoever. For information address Gallery Books Subsidiary Rights Department, 1230 Avenue of the Americas, New York, NY 10020

First Gallery Books trade paperback edition June 2019

GALLERY BOOKS and colophon are registered trademarks of Simon & Schuster, Inc.

For information about special discounts for bulk purchases, please contact Simon & Schuster Special Sales at 1-866-506-1949 or business@simonandschuster.com

The Simon & Schuster Speakers Bureau can bring authors to your live event. For more information or to book an event contact the Simon & Schuster Speakers Bureau at 1-866-248-3049 or visit our website at www.simonspeakers.com.

Manufactured in the United States of America

1 3 5 7 9 10 8 6 4 2

Library of Congress Cataloging-in-Publication Data is available.

ISBN 978-1-5011-1794-7 (hardcover)
ISBN 978-1-5011-1795-4
ISBN 978-1-5011-1797-8 (ebook)

Photo of Miranda on pg. 170 courtesy of James Shubinski.

i'd like to dedicate
this book to the
most important
Person in my Life...
myself.

DISCLAMER

This book has a lot of cut outs and activities wear you draw in the book. So you need to get a back up book. Go Buy another one rite now so you can cut this 1 up and drawl in it and have a extra 1 that is perfeck.

Also, im NOT responsible 4 injury to person or property as a result of using my good advice in this book. So dont sue me cuz im NOT that type of girl.

Table of Contents

INTroductioN.

welcome to my selp helf book. in this book I will supply you with the best advice in the world on becoming a better person. By the end of this book your love life, career, self esteem, finances, health, etc will all be perfect. Your welcome,

ABOUTME

i was borned on December 24, one day be4 Jesus so you know, just saying. Right away they knew i was destined for grateness because i beat the placenta out of the tookie.

As I grew older my fans realized my many talents such as acting, modeling, book writing and such as.

Dont belive me? just look at this modeling pic from when i was a baby.

Being Born

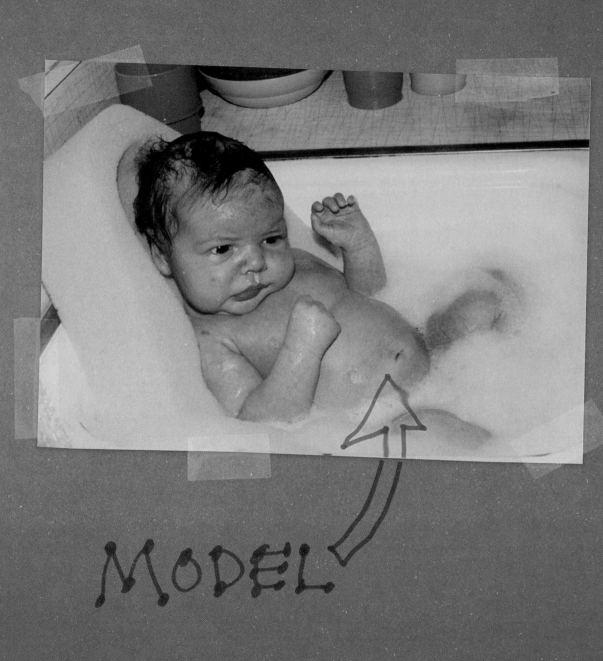

MODEL

LOVE

in This chapter i will Tech you how to How 2 conker LOVE and how 2 get a Boyfrind but not a girlfrind cuz im Not a Lebonese.

QUALITIES to LOOK FOR.

Attracive

Pretty

Hairs

Rich

This

Famus
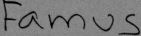

QUaLities To Have.

Cute

Bootiful

Atractive

Sensual

Pritty

5

L♥VE LANGUAGES

Every1 shows L♥ve through 1 of the 5 L♥ve languages. Hear R the 5 languages and how they R used.

EYE LANGUAGE

i see you

yeh rite

BODY LANGUAGE

Come here

COME HERE

Get A BoyFrind Kit

Binoculars

Perfume

Black clothes

Rubber gloves

Handcuffs

Camera with Night vision

Flashlite

8

Writing A Love Note

Nothing is more romantic than slipping a man a love note. So slip a letter onto his pillow when hes not home, or under the Bathroom stall while he is peepee-ing. Heres some essamples of love notes.

ROSES are RED
VIOLETS ARE BLUE
STOP STALKING TO the MAIL LADY
IM WATCHING YOU!

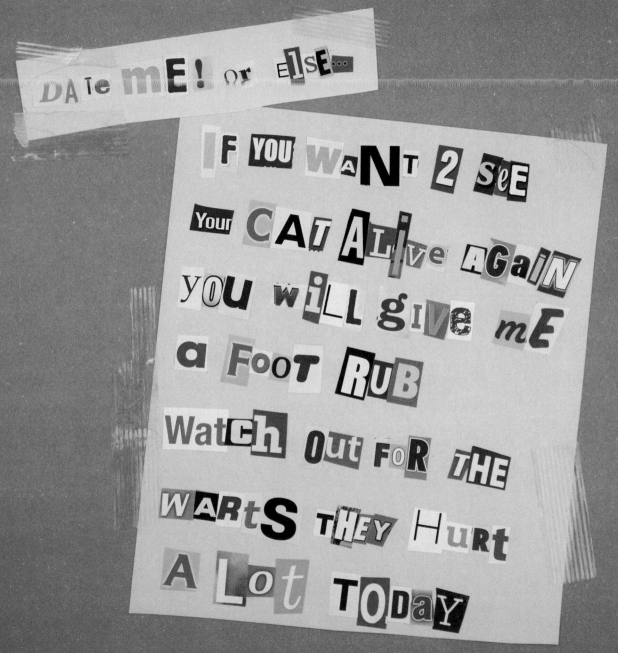

11

Levels of a relationship

Level 1 stranger.

Level 2 mine.

Level 3 Bae

Level 4 Husband

Level 5 servant

Level 6 Prisoner

Level 7 widow

12

My uncle wrote out the difrent bases in touching in relatchonships

1ST

Before you start running the bases, you need to be sure you're ready to play the game in the first place. I'm talking training, practice, a little t-ball if you know what I mean.

FIRST BASE
First contact/first look. Love a first sight? Yes. First base is staring. Could be across the room, through a window. Lots of options.

SECOND BASE
Base two: the massage. A gentle rub on the neck, back or shoulder can express your feelings. This is a great way to connect with someone, I use it on my customers all the time.

HOME RUN
This is your first kiss. It's like eating the last plumb of the season. Your lips gush with juice as it runs down its skin and your tongue runs across the tender flesh bursting with flavor. It's like that.

THIRD BASE
This base is cuddling. Unless you're family you should wait to cuddle until you get married.

2ND

3RD

BASES IN A RELATIONSHIP

13

First Date

Movies

The nice thing about movies is its quiet so its a grate place to talk and get to know each other.

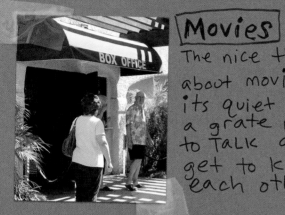

Uncles House

Very private place where you can play with your Daddy saddle.

CONVERSATION TOPICS

- yourself
- How many kids do you want?
- How much money do you have?
- what diseases run in yor family?
- Types of Yarn
- Do you mind genital warts

First Date Eddikate

3 ways to play hard to get.

it's good to act uninterested in your First date to Leave him wanting more.

① PHYSICALLY - Punch them, hit them, spit near them, Pull a hair.

② VERBALLY - tell them they are ugly

③ EMOTIONALLY - act ~~un-inter~~ uninterested and bored to hurt their feelings

marriage

Now that you've been on a date, your ready for marriage.

marriage is about 3 things

① A dress.

② a cake.

③ making other people jealous.

Wedding Vows

its important 2 write your own vows Because traditional vows have promises you wont Be able to keep. I wrote some 4 you to use.

i, miranda take you, Bae...to Be my husband. I promise to Be the Best person in this relatchonship. For Im Better your worse im richer, your poorer your sick im in health as Long as you shall Live.

Amen.

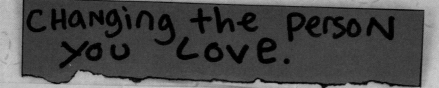

Changing the Person you Love.

People often say that you cant change a person. That is not true. People who say that are just lazy. Hear are some ways you can change someone

NOT Thoughtful?

Talk to them in their sleep to influence there thoughts

Never Buys you gifts?

Buy things for yourself with his credit card

EXpressiNG YOUR FeeLiNGS is HARD.

iF you or someoNe you No has
ProBLeMs expressing itseLF
Just Look at this List of
FeeLings and check Boxes
that match you Best.

☐ SAD   ☐ hungry   ☐ sticky
☐ happy   ☐ awake   ☐ singy
☐ excited   ☐ ok   ☐ cry-y
☐ angry   ☐ asleep   ☐ FuLL
☐ depressed   ☐ wet   ☐ Loud
☐ Bored   ☐ tired   ☐ other

how to cuddle ♥

Back to Back

spoon

in the womb

Christian

cuddeling is important in a marriage because it's when you touch for the first time. hear are the cuddeling positchons.

69

Sharing air

the uncle

21

Breaking up.

YouTube Video: Great way to get more views

Twitter: Use hashtags like #BreakingUp or #OnTheProwl

Text Message

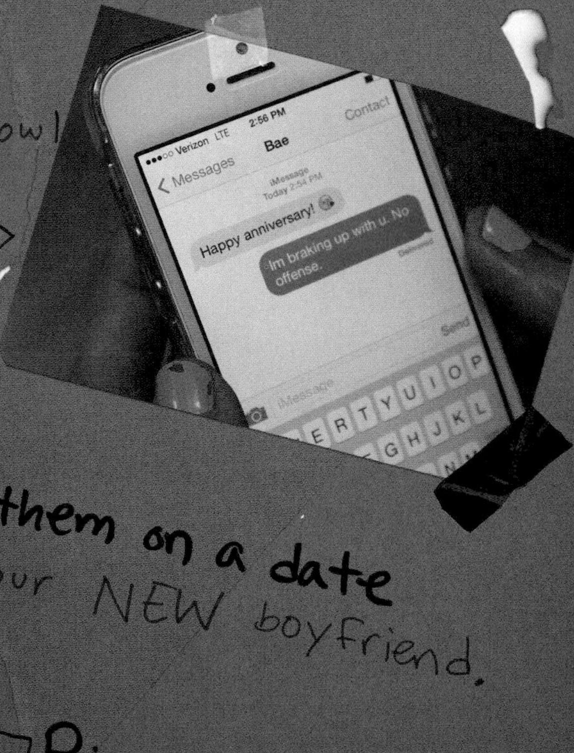

Invite them on a date with your NEW boyfriend.

Ring Box

HEARTACHE

someTimes the boy will brake up with you. if this happens You will need to learn how to get over a broken heart because no one likes being around Sad People. its anoying. How you get over a broken heart is to Stop being sad. Easy.

or get revenge. (see next page 4 details.

Getting Revenge

- [ ] spit in his drink
- [ ] kick a bush in his yard
- [ ] catch a fly and let it go in his bedroom (make sure its a loud one)
- [ ] put hair in his mouth
- [ ] crunch up all his cereal and put it back in the box
- [ ] Dont talk to him
- [ ] Kiss something in front of him
- [ ] cut the erasers off his pencils

LOVE QUIZ

WHAT KIND OF BAE ARE YOU?
(results on next page)

where would you go on a date?
a. uncles house - 3 points
b. beach - 1 point
c. nothing - 2 point

how do you kiss?
a. on mouth - 1 point
b. on hand - 3 points
c. hairs - 2 points

what's your type?
a. bad boy - 1 point
b. model - 2 points
c. that guy at the park - 3 points

what kind of pet do u want?
a. dog - 2 points
b. snake - 1 points
c. ant farm - 3 points

what do you like for dinner?
a. spagehtti - 1 point
b. celery - 2 points
c. salami - 3 points

LOVE QUIZ RESULTS

5-9 points SLUTTY BAE
You are a SLUT. Put ur tongue back in your mouth and stop being
so inapropriate. You need prayer.

10-14 points BORING BAE
You are a boring bae. you will probably never keep a lover
because u are too boring and they will leave you. no offense

15-20 points SENUAL BAE
You know how to keep a man. you are almost a slut but keep it
holy enough to be a good lady.

25-30 points Miranda
you are perfect.

TALENT

In this chapter i will
Tech you how to
Have a talent
cuz you probly
dont have one.

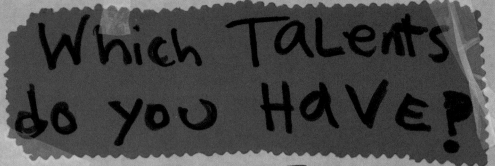

Which Talents do you Have?

Check the Talents you Have

- ☐ singing
- ☐ acting
- ☐ Dancing
- ☐ model
- ☐ magichen
- ☐ drawing
- ☐ dressing up cats
- ☐ eating
- ☐ gardening
- ☐ photo making
- ☐ cooking
- ☐ jumping

- ☐ Loom bracelets
- ☐ sleeping
- ☐ cursive
- ☐ swimming
- ☐ whistling

Some people have 3 or 4 of these. I have them all so in case you dont have a talents i will tech you some.

SINGING

"Singing" is a talent that sounds like talking but with more singing.

Singing is my #1 talent so im the best person to tech you aboutit. in the next few pages i will tech you how to be a grate singer

vibrato is that shaking sound
your voice makes. Shake a part
of your body and it shakes
your voice . i shake my head.

The BIGGER the shake,
the bigger the vibrato

Learning MUSIC

Learning music is important because
you need to learn how to learn
music. some people
will give you music
that looks like this

That makes no sense so just use a piano.

↑
Lowest NOTE
You can sing

↑
Chopsticks

↑
high Note i
can hit but
you probly cant

*if you dont have a piano just pretend.

DANCING

DANCING IS A GREAT TALENT TO HAVE BECAUSE YOU CAN DO IT TO MUSIC OR NOT. HEAR ARE SOME GOOD DANCE MOVES

← MOON WALK

SINGLE LADY →

THE ← WORM

TWERKING
← scan to wach how to twerk appropriatly

IN order to dance goodly
you need good techneek.
Ballet is the Best way
to getit

BALLet Positchons

1st   2nd   3rd   Splits

repeat.

35

NOW YOU KNOW HOW TO DANCE BUT

BEWARE

dancing can be dangerous. some dancing is very inna- propriate and can make others Lust.

Dance moves to stay away from

| Michael Jackson | The Twerk | The prom | Pole dance |

Drawing

Drawing is another good talent to have.

① ○   ② ○   ③

④   ⑤   ⑥

Hear is how to draw a person.

ACTING

For This Talent You have to be good with your Face. Try these etspressions.

 happy

 sad

 confused

 healthy

 disappointed

 smart

 Pritty

 titked off

 Tired

MY UNCLE TALKS ABOUT HEADSHOTS

As Miranda's manager, I know the importance and technique of getting good headshots. Lighting and costume are good, but capturing attitude and avant guard moments can be the difference between an okay headshot and getting the role.

It's also important to keep your headshots current. That's why I take lots of pictures of Miranda every day.

— Tim

MAGIC

MAGIC works By Lying.

step one: Lie
its not going to disapear.

step two - Lie
Theres nothing over there.

step three - Lie.
it did not disapear.

step 4 - Lie.
it is under my shirt.

41

Dressing Up CATS

This is a gr8 skill because it makes cats better and more like people.

42

Talent Awards

Cut out the award that you earned.

Singing

Draws Good

acting

Majic

Other

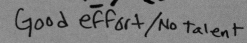

Good effort/No talent

43

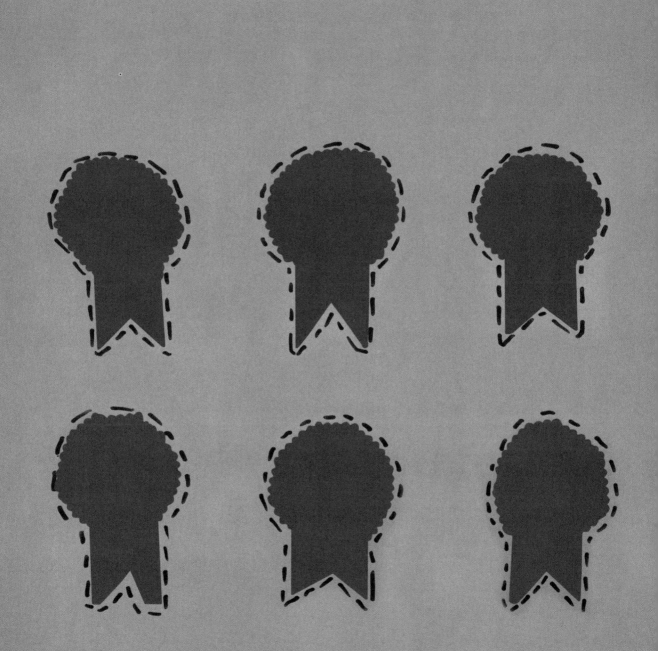

Fatchen

its important to be Fatchenable because the most popular people in the world have a good sense of Fatchen.

Clothes say a lot about a person. For example: "I am not naked!" or "I am wearing clothes."

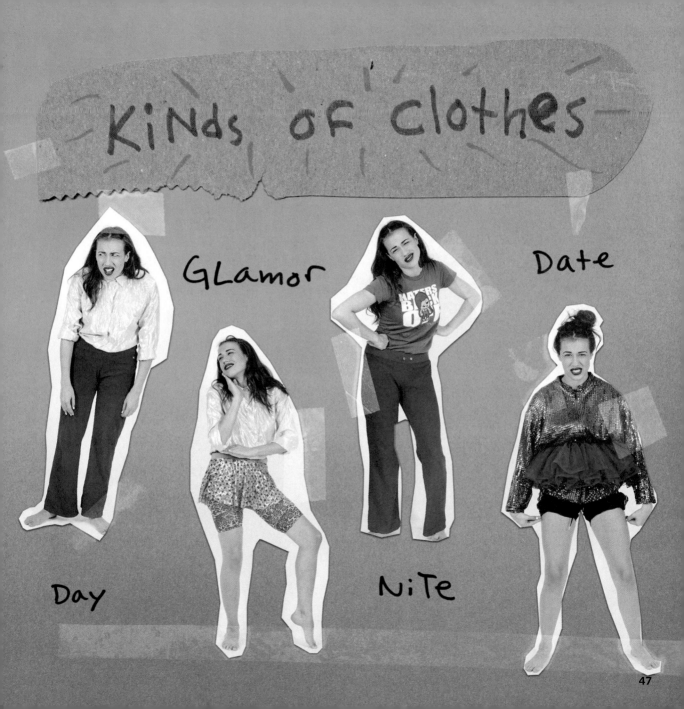

Kinds of clothes

GLamor

Date

Day

Nite

47

shoes are the window
to the soul.

Business

Fun

Slut

Hungry

other.

Know what your shoes mean.

MAKE UP

Make up is good Because
it tricks people to think
You look difrent than you
do. Now i will teach
you about different kinds
of makeup and how 2 use it

49

EYE BROWS

NATURAL

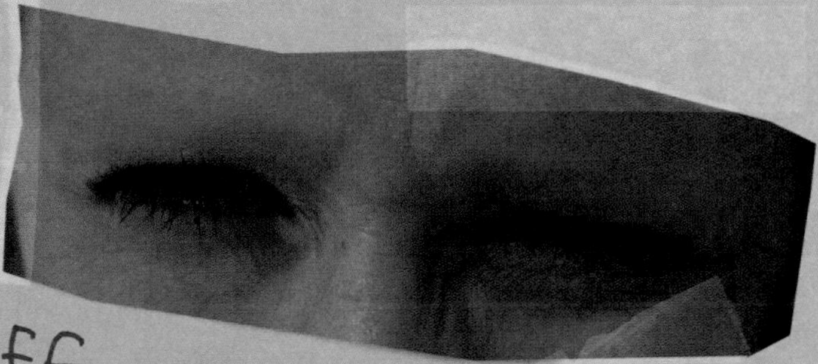

Shave them off

draw them on.

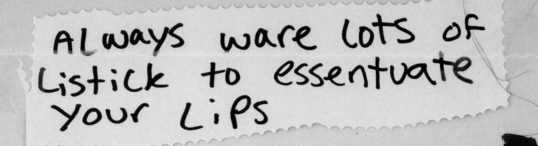

Always ware lots of Listick to essentuate your Lips

Listick

put it here

51

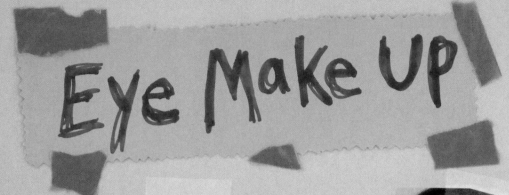

Eyeshadews R Fun cuz its
like facepaint kind of.
hear are some looks for
you 2 try.

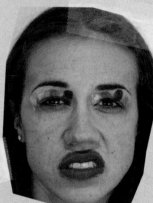

Cat eye

Rainbow

smokey

Sprinkles

52

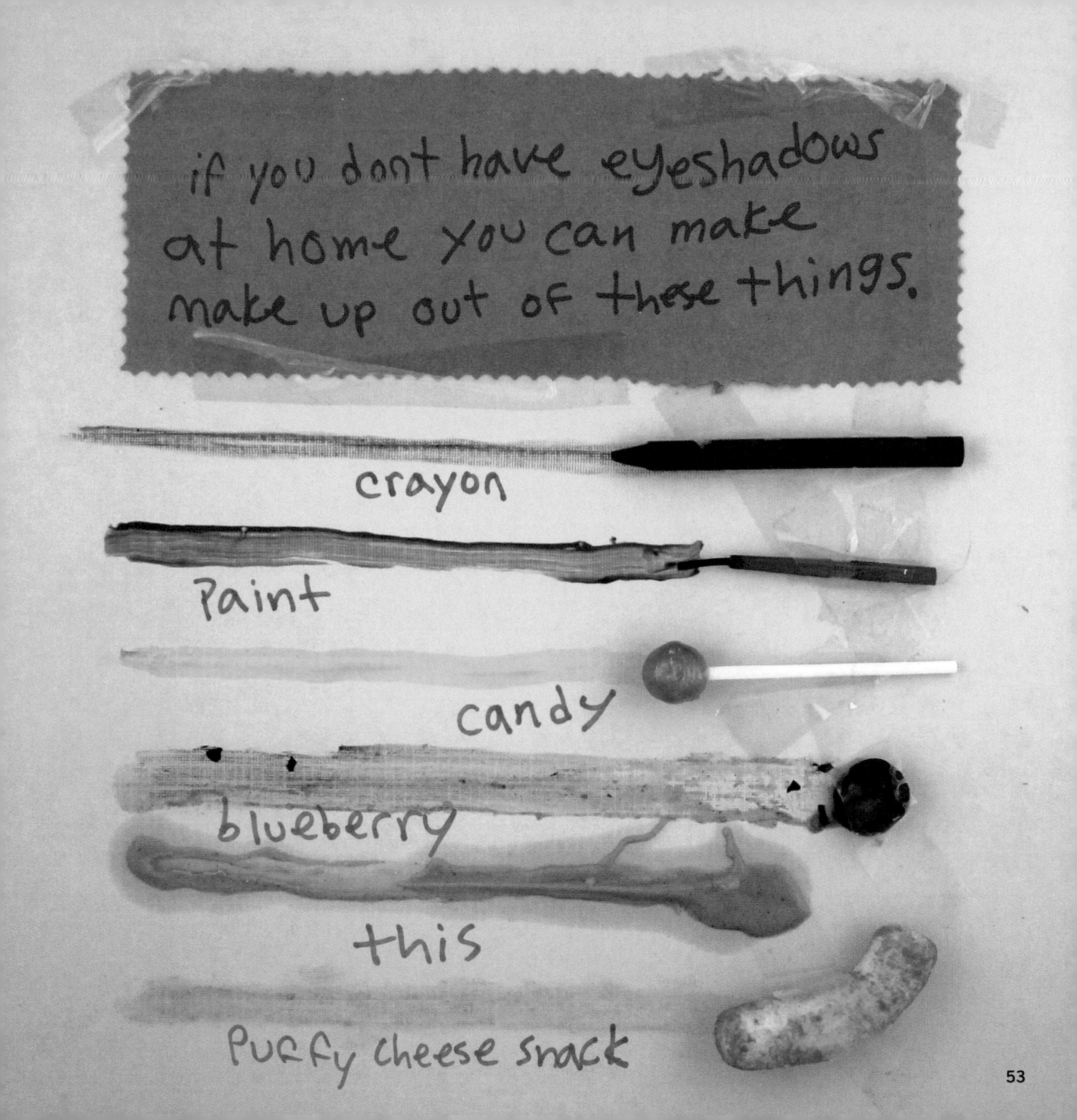

if you dont have eyeshadows at home you can make make up out of these things.

crayon

Paint

candy

blueberry

this

Purry cheese snack

53

OTHER EYE MAKE-UPS

EYE-LINER

eye liner is pokey and dangerous. i do not recomend.

MASCARA

mascara is pokey and dangerous. i do not recomend

FAKE EYELATCHES

Fake eyelatches are pokey and dangerous 4 your eyes. hear are other ways you can use them.

mustash →

Finger wigs →

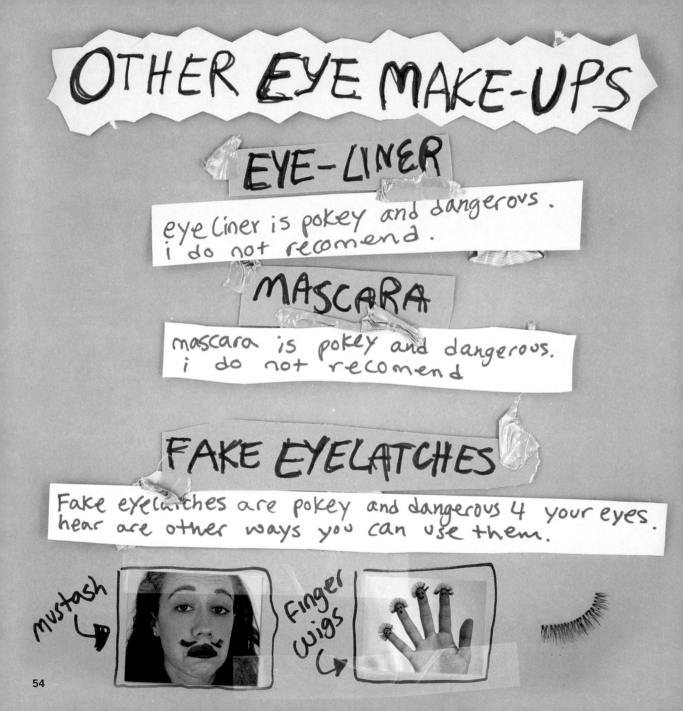

55

STAINS

Grape juice, skettios, soap, these are all things that stain. DONT even worry about it. I got your back girl.

stain

Fix your stain with..

broach   scarf   hand   paper

Accessories

you put these on your clothes and skin to look more fancier hear are my favorit accessorries

Hats   Necklace   braslet   socks   bag   bows

rings   scarf   stickers   earrings purses tape balloons

hairties   String   animals   Swords   box headbands

Make your own jewelry

Jewelry is expensive so hear i will show you how you can make your own.

Tape Bracelet

hair Ring

hanger earrings

tooth neklace

PORN

There are lots of diffrent kinds of porn. The pitcher below shows a few esamples.

lots of skins

satan juice

Tookie

chestical crack

creases

other

60

ANTi PoRN UNiCoRN

i noticed you looking at my unicorn on the last page. his name is anti-porn unicorn and he helps get rid of porn in the world by poking it with his horn. now you can be an anti-porn unicorn too! Just cut out the horn on the next page and tape it to your head like this.

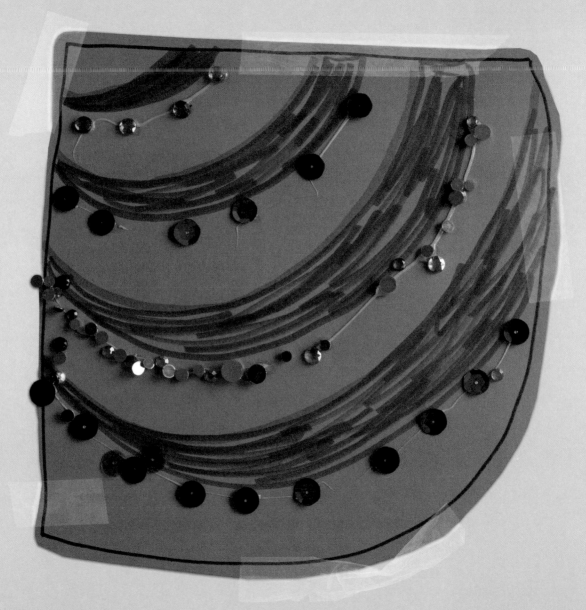

63

MoDELing

Now that you look fachonable, you need to learn how to act fachonable. This is called being a model. I will teach you how to look like a model. if you are ugly turn the page.

MODEL POSES

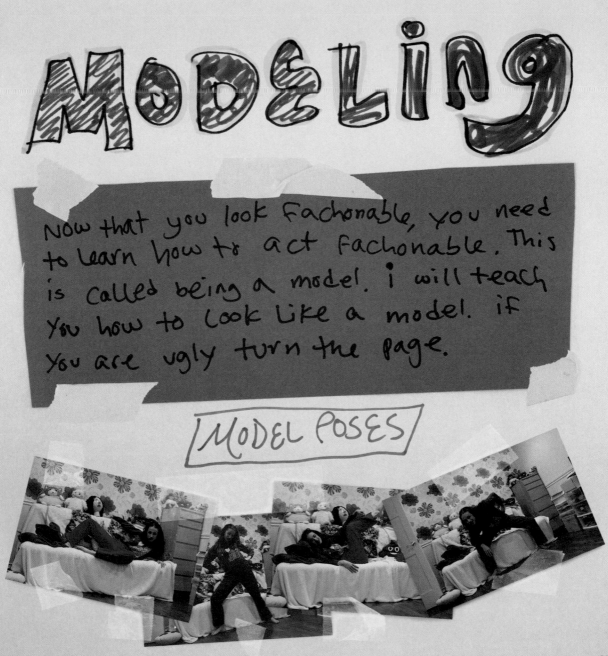

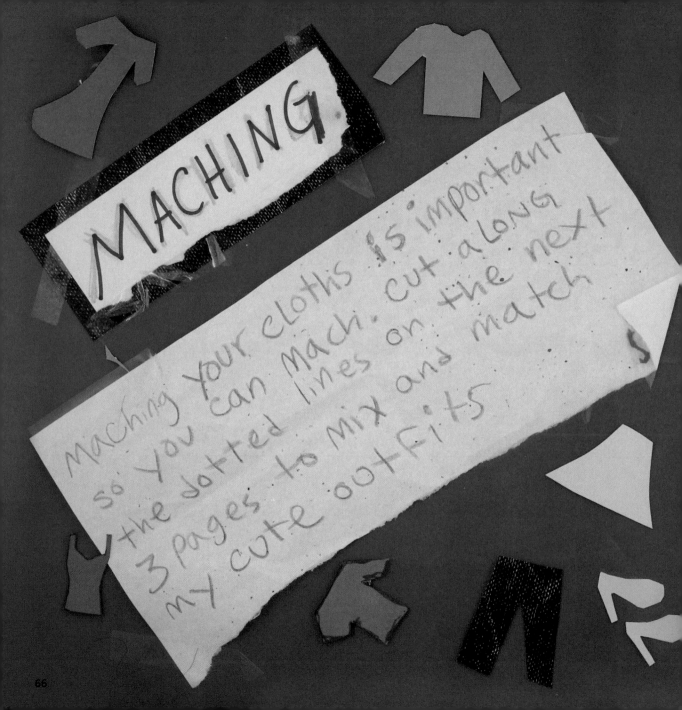

MACHING

Maching your cloths is important so you can machi. cut along the dotted lines on the next 3 pages to mix and match my cute ootfits

66

67

71

72

First you will need to write a Resume. This is a peace of paper that says the jobs you did in the past

- - - - - - - - - - -

Look at this sample resume and see some of the commen mistakes most people make.

Becca Thompson

OBJECTIVE
To find a secretarial job at a law office.

WORK EXPERIENCE

2013 to present	Sales Clerk, Stanford Fine Socks Help customers and run front register
2012 to 2013	Marketing Technician, E.L.M. Telecommunications Made cold-calls and sales inquiries
2009 to 2012	Usher, Clementine Theaters Helped people find their seats, served concessions

EDUCATION

B.A.	Philosophy Golden Leaf University, 2012
Diploma	Green River High School Richmond, Virginia 2008

HONORS/AWARDS
Graduated Cum Laude
First runner up for national mock trials
E.L.M.'s top closing telemarketer for January

SKILLS
Excel, Word, Computer Networking, advanced anatomy sketch rendering, filing

REFERENCES

Cary Federman	Manager E.L.M. Telecommunications
Marry Valentine	Manager Clementine Theaters
Carl White	Professor GLU

Problems With Resume

Too much Blank space you should pack it up with more Bragging.

This is a Boring job. Show motivation By saying movie star, astronaut or cat Breeder.

this part is Boring. No offense

Use prittier font Like comic sans

too much to read

use pink ink to stand out.

thes skills aren't very good. you should Lie.

No stickers.

75

INTERVIEWS

The next step in getting a job is to go on a interview. This is when you talk to someone about yourself. Hear are some tips to help you get the job

SHOW UP LATE

This helps you look more important and like you have Better things to do.

DIRECT EYE CONTACT

Dont Blink or look away. This shows that You're paying attention.

USE POSTERS

visual aids are very important. See next page for poster ideas.

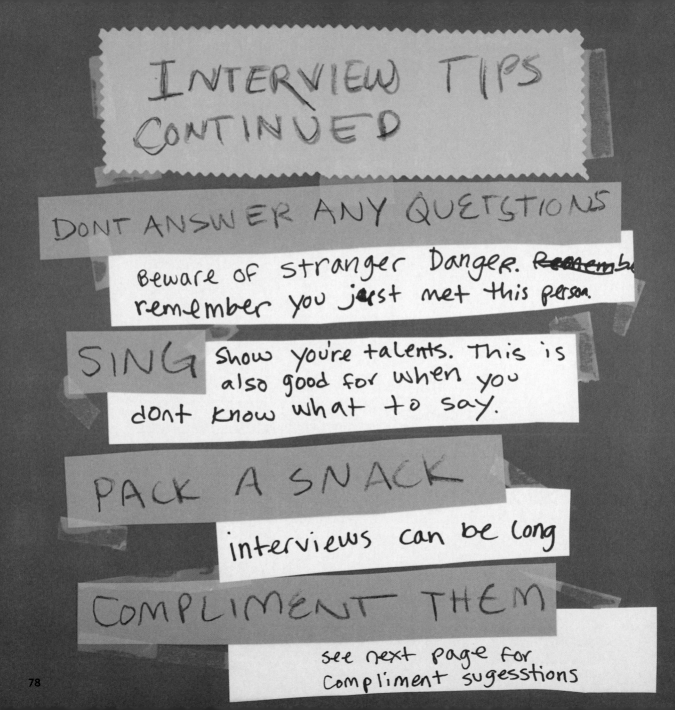

INTERVIEW TIPS CONTINUED

DONT ANSWER ANY QUESTIONS

Beware of stranger Danger. ~~Reeeember~~ remember you just met this person.

SING

Show you're talents. This is also good for when you dont know what to say.

PACK A SNACK

interviews can be long

COMPLIMENT THEM

see next page for compliment sugesstions

Make Yourself Irreplaceable

UNPLUG all the telephones But your own.

Keep all the toilet paper in your office

Steal everyones lunch

Do the Bare minimum to
keep your job.
Do the Bare minimum
slower and keep the
job Twice as long.

83

Work is Boring. Hear
are some posters you can
Blow up 2 stay motivated.

Posters

Tape pieces
of paper together
to make a Big
poster

example

85

GETTING Fired.

Tip 1: Never get fired.

Tip 2: Quit Before they fire you

Tip3: If they tell you you are Fired, dont Listen.

GETTING REVENGE

- Use the toilet paper you stole.

- De-friend them on social media.

- Never speak to them again.

- Get a new job. (go Back to page 1 of this chapter)

-

RAT RACE

Use what you have lernt to solve this maze.

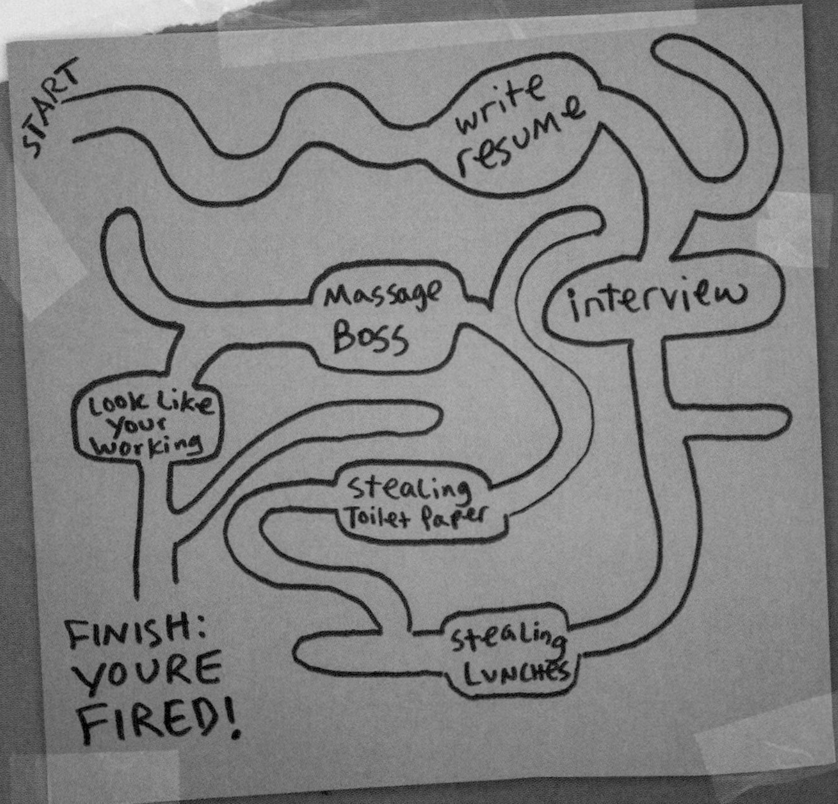

This chapter is about how 2 save money. 1st sTep is to get money (see career chapter.) iF you dont Like working hear are some ways to make money without a job.

FIND IN COUCH
Extra Bonus! sometimes you find food.

GET A RICH BAE.
make sure he is also famus.

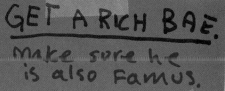

ASK MOM
if she says no, find her purse and take it anyway.

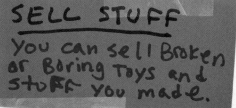

SELL STUFF
You can sell Broken or Boring Toys and stuff you made.

HOW to make MONEY

Another way to make money is to make money. You can use the examples on the next page and cut out you're very own money.

$ $ $

92

93

FINALLY

There is one way to get money without working, searching, dating, asking, cutting things out, or any of these kinds of things. You can actually get FREE MONEY. its using a little thing i like to call credit cards

95

My uncle knows a lot about investing so he wrote this. So their you go.

I'M GLAD THAT YOU ASKED ABOUT THIS BECAUSE I HAVE JUST INVESTED IN AN OPPORTUNITY THAT YOU MIGHT BE INTERESTED IN ALSO. FOR JUST THE SMALL START-UP PRICE OF 179.99 YOU CAN BECOME A CONSULTANT AND SALES PERSON FOR THESE FANTASTIC VITAMINS.

BASICALLY IF YOU SIGN UP WITH ME TODAY, YOU'LL BE ABLE TO SELL VITAMINS FOR PROFIT AND YOU CAN RECRUIT NEW CONSULTANTS AND YOU'LL GET A PERCENTAGE OF THEIR SALES. I GET A PERCENTAGE OF YOUR SALES JUST LIKE THE GUY WHO RECRUITED ME GETS A PERCENTAGE OF MY SALES

IN FACT IF YOUR RECRUITS GET NEW RECRUITS YOU GET A PERCENTAGE OF THEIR SALES. AND SO ON, AND SO ON. EVERYBODY MAKES MONEY TOGETHER! SOUNDS GREAT, RIGHT?

I KNOW WHAT YOU'RE THINKING, "JIM, THIS SOUNDS LIKE JUST ANOTHER PYRAMID SCHEME." WHAT? NO. WORKS COMPLETELY DIFFERENT. I'LL DRAW A DIAGRAM TO MAKE IT MORE CLEAR.

ETC.

THEIR SALES TEAM

YOUR SALES TEAM

YOU

MONEY FLOW

MONEY FLOW

Look out for good Deals

50¢ or 5 for Just $2

ALL TOILET BRUSHES
BUY 10
GET 11th
FREE!

HAIR GROW
SUPLEMEN
FOR MEN
30% MORE

COUPONS

CUT out these coupons To use

30% OFF TOYS

½ off Lipstick

FRee Cat !

Extra meat when buying meat

Buy 1 Get 3 Sodas

Name your Price

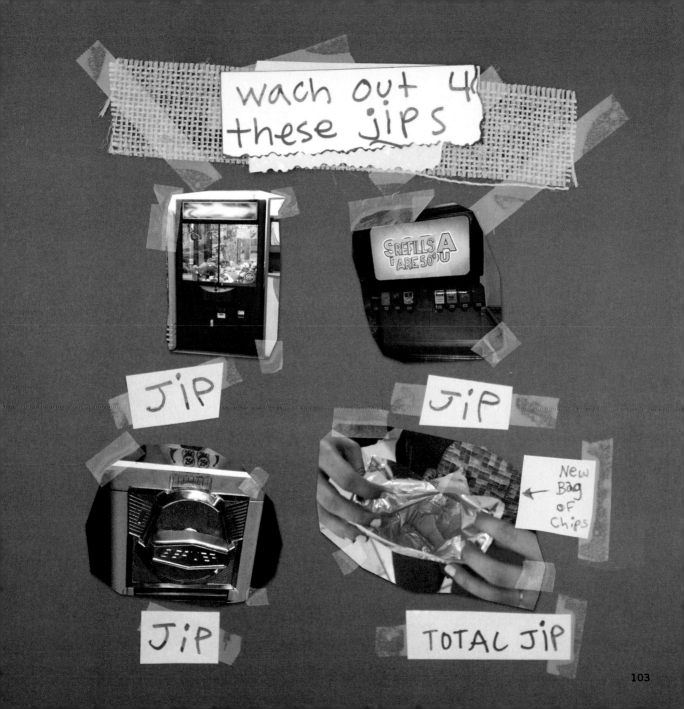

103

Making Money Grow

A Lot of people talk about making money grow. They are Liars. I've tried it and it doesnt work at all.

FAIL↵

What is the value of a dollar?

Easy. 100 pennies. next quetchon.

TRY some of these Free activities

Go to the POUND

its like the zoo but Free and Better cuz they change out the animals every week

Birthday party

Find a Birthday party at a park. They dont know you so they wont expect a present. Free cake. Free Food. Free Jumpy house. Free pinyata.

Wach TV

Doesnt cost anything and you can turn it up loud enough so you cant hear your mom telling you wat to do.

Road trip

Flying is so espensive so just trick someone into driving you anywhear you want. its Fun and Free

WHAT CAN YOU GET

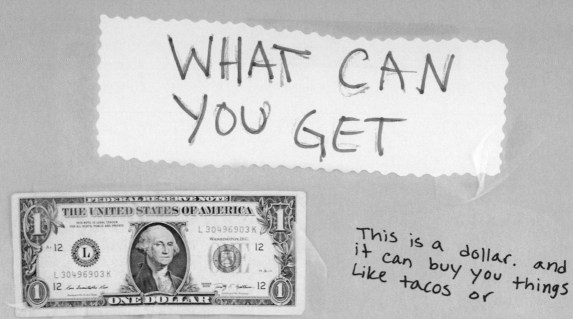

This is a dollar. and it can buy you things Like tacos or

i never seen one of these they probly dont even exist

This is good to get bouncy Balls or gum.

Tip For waiter

This coin is too Fat for how much its worth.

Pointless. throw away.

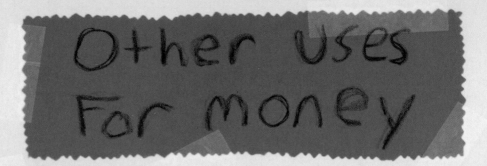

Other Uses For Money

Fix a wiggly table

Cleaning out teeth

A top (perfect toy for Babys)

writing a note.

LeTs PLaY A gamE

Connect the dots!

its a mystery...

What could it Be?

HINTS
① it has to do with this chapter
② its the symbol 4 money
③ its a "5" with a line through it.

109

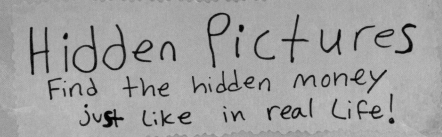

Hidden Pictures
Find the hidden money just like in real life!

Be smart.
The end.

INTERNET

its important to have the skill of the internet cuz everything on the internet is true. Come with me as i unfold how 2 internet the best.

Before you get started online you need to learn to speak the language.

LOL - laugh out loud
WERK - to werk
selfie - a pitchur
Yolo - You only live once
OMG - Oh my ~~gracias~~ ~~gratious~~ ~~gracius~~ gracias
FML = fogrot my lunch
LMAO - let me ask others
BAE - (See piture 1)
FAIL - Falling And Internet Laughter
ILYSM - i love yogurt sometimes
gr8 - growling and 8

Piture 1 →

Social Media

social media is a great place to take pitchurs of your food, poke people, make people jealis, and brag. *see exampels below*

mirandasingsofficial

mirandasingsofficial

Miranda Sings
@MirandaSings

I always new I was famous because people look at me some times.

mirandasingsofficial

♥ 38620 likes
mirandasingsofficial Me and my number 1 fan after my show

Miranda Sings
Posted by Miranda Sings

hi
13,434 Likes · 1,068 Comments

👍 Like   💬 Comment   ➦ Share

♥ 33620 likes
mirandasingsofficial Filmed a video with @flula today

Miranda Sings
@MirandaSings

I'm so glad I've changed so many lives. #blessed #livingTheDeeam #famous #Obamacare

115

Social Media Platforms

My stupid Lawyer, said i cant put actual names of social medias in my Book. so i disguised their names so you wont know wich is wich.

BLitter — For Fangirling & hashtagging

BLuetube — For people to get Famous

BLinstagram — For showing your food and Face.

BLacebook — For old people

BLapchat — For pitchurs that need to disappear (poo, panties, strangers,)

BLine — For videos you want to wach over and over and over and over

BLumber — i dont get it.

Video Ideas

CHALLENGES

it doesnt matter what the challenge is. it will get views. so eat a spider, burn off your hairs, take a slushi Bath, something respecktable like that. People like waching you throw up. Almost dying is Better.

TUTORIALS

Teach People how to do something online cuz obviously your opinion is more valuble then Professionals @ things like fashon and cooking

COLLABORATIONS

Take advantage of other youtubers By making videos with them and stealing their subscribers

MUSIC VIDEOS

Sing a cover of someone elses song. This is gr8 Because you dont have to Be talented or creative. just do it & people will watch

Tips for going viral.

CLEAN

Before

After

use good Liting.

Viral Videos.

↑
Camera

↑
Computer

↑
Person

↑
Snack

WHAT YOU NEED

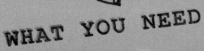
viral videos are videos that spread relly Fast. Like warts.

viral videos I made

Voice Lesson

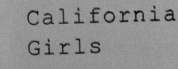

California Girls

Do You want to Build a snowman

Taking Pitchurs and putting them online is very important. The Better you look, the more likes you will get. Just like in real life.

Things you can Post to ~~BL~~ instagram

Face

Food

Animals

Shoes

Coffee

Quotes

DO YOU KNOW WHAT THY DO ON HALLOWEEN?

THEY KILL CATS!!

A selfie is a pitchur of Yourself or other things

good Angles

OVER

UNDER

FRONT

FACE

Aim

Phone

Extend

Person
(You)

122

BLitteR

Blitter is a great way to TELL people what your doing at all times. you can update them on important things in life like if your cold or Bored.

GAiNiNG Followers

Miranda Sings @MirandaSings · 4m
EVERY1 FOLLOW ME RITE NOW OR ELSE U WILL BE CURST
1.1K   2.4K

Miranda Sings @MirandaSings · 4m
im not kiding folow me right now i need more followers and if u don't follow me i will break ur arm or worse i will spit
1.2K   2.4K

Miranda Sings @MirandaSings · 6m
you better all folow me right now or i swear i will find u and u will regret it so hard.
1.1K   2.3K

There are **2** good ways to gain followers.

① Threaten

② Nag

Miranda Sings @MirandaSings · 2m
@tyleroakley follow meh x8
107   225

Miranda Sings @MirandaSings · 2m
@tyleroakley follow meh x7
123   271

Miranda Sings @MirandaSings · 2m
@tyleroakley follow meh x6
127   293

Miranda Sings @MirandaSings · 2m
@tyleroakley follow meh x5
149   347

Miranda Sings @MirandaSings · 2m
@tyleroakley follow meh x4
152   384

Miranda Sings @MirandaSings · 2m
@tyleroakley follow meh x3
164   421

Miranda Sings @MirandaSings · 2m
@tyleroakley follow meh x2
186   443

Miranda Sings @MirandaSings · 2m
@tyleroakley follow meh x1
208   474

Be sure to BYtweet with hashtags

@MirandaSings
I ruined my panties. #SundayFunday #sorrynotsorry

@MirandaSings
Sticky parts are on my skin today. Not my fault.
#WhatColorIsTheDress

@MirandaSings
I love a sturdy crock. #blessed #winning

@MirandaSings
If I accidentaly pour juice all over my moms computer
when I was mad & it broke, how can I fix it before she
finds out? #Askingforafriend

@MirandaSings
If at first you don't succeed then give up ur not good at it.
#follow #globalwarming

@MirandaSings
My mom came in my room today and I was like no #me

Hashtags are used to explain your pitchur. Also to brag.

#MYSELF

#YOLO

#KONY 2012

#BLessed

#MadAtMyUncle

Blacebook

My mom and uncle use
~~Kace~~ ᴮᴸ Facebook all the time
So im going to let them
write a few things.
They Better Not Be boring
Or annoying or i wont let
them in the Book im not even
kidding.

I love **BI**acebook. it's a great place to connect with old friends from grade school and say happy Birthday to people. I also really enjoy being poked.

Martha posted a lovely photo of a kitten on my face wall last week and Ruby wrote a comment on it that was simply hilarious. Did you see that? I can't remember what it said now... something about cats I think. I remember it ended with "lol" or something clever like that.

BIacebook is also a great place to create events and start group messages about upcoming craft parties. Although, Ruby wasn't invited to Lisa's scrabble event last week. I hope she is doing well after that. Everyone loves my posts about Miranda. Yesterday I was given 3 likes and 5 pokes! Such fun! ♡

~Bethany

Here's what my Uncle thinks of Blacebook.........

DO NOT TRUST BLACEBOOK!

YEAH, I USED TO USE BLACEBOOK, THEN THEY CHANGED THEIR SECURITY SETTINGS. I REPOSTED ALL KINDS OF STUFF TO GET THEM TO CHANGE IT BACK BUT IT WAS NO USE. NOW EVERY AD, EVERY POST IS ABOUT THINGS THAT I AM INTERESTED IN. PERSONAL THINGS THAT THEY COULD NOT KNOW UNLESS THEY WERE SPYING ON ME THROUGH MY OWN WEBCAM. OH, SURE, HACK MY E-MAIL AND STEAL MY IDENTITY. THAT'D BE GOOD. NO THANK YOU BLACEBOOK!

BLapchat

i Love this Social medid cuz
you can try out new
hairstyles and LOOKS.

AND if you take a pic
OF something you dont
Like it disappears!
heres a example of a
Pitchur im glad Disappeared

BLine

Bline is a place where you scream a lot, say bad words, or be rasist. i choose to scream. what do you choose? circle one...

SCREAM   BAD WORDS   RASIST

BLUMBLER

im Not even kidding
i don't get it
at all.

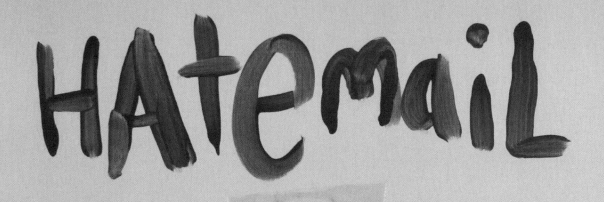

HATEMAIL

Hatemail is something you will get from Haters on your social medias. its relly rude and ANOYING. the next few pages are hatemails i have gotted on my social medias. (close eyes while reading. its very dangerus.)

134

HATEMAIL

MisterGolwin MD
well now my ears have aids

Kristorgyles1982
The entire video I was wondering how she was covering her monster size penis

dontstepbeleevn5
no, ' no no no no................STOP SINGING LISTEN TO YOURSELF AND COMPARE IT TO REAL SINGERS U SOND LIKE UR POOING!!!!!!!!!!!!

f1oridatrou6lemkr
BEEP YOU MIRDANA

Poppxd4ddy
She's uglier than he'll

MsSupTe55o
Thumbs up if you only clicked on this video because you thought she was going to chocck :)

HATemail

xxxgothicks69
I had to stab myself with a pencil to dull the pain this video gave me

he110kewlgang42
wwwww is this botch *beep* im fur real? Nasty get the *beep* away from this kids you look like some retraded rapest and u sing like *beep*! If i ever see this hoe *beep* retard ima knock you out smash your face in that sand and stomp on your head till u shut the *beep* up for good that was so bad i couldn't even listen to the whole thing!
Sad face… my ear r burned

InsameMasheen5
Oh, I'm sorry, I couldn't hear you over the sound of me puking

mik mccornix
uhygtykbjvycryfdxefgxdrgerfgftcr5yfr5hfrr4t5 *beep* you go to hell and stay there forever

HATEMAIL

Ma661Nawly
What the *beep* you tryna do to people dread? You in some kinda *beep* in mad people home Iowa? LAWD HAVE MERCY...... GIRL HUSH YOUR BLASTE MOUTH NAW..... setups....only squak squak squak squak you a *beep* parrot....HUSH!

Ch1po4u5
My dad came in and I switched to porn because it was easier to explain

pr1nce55pa9s
seriously wot is rong wiv ur lip? and wot is rong wiv ur voice? u need to sort urself out and get a life, i am NOT a hater coz u make me and my family laugh our heads off. but if we r goin by talent, i do hate ya, i am a hater! stop postin these videos and just do sumink else!! ur ruining my life!!

Re5pectab1eBeeuTay
1st of you can't sing, nor like a black woman. You don't have to be big to sing like a bigger black women. you cant sing so stop. And your stupid cause black woman don't move their head, it's called having soul, which you will never have. This answer is from a serious woman (a serious and now angry black woman) unlike you.

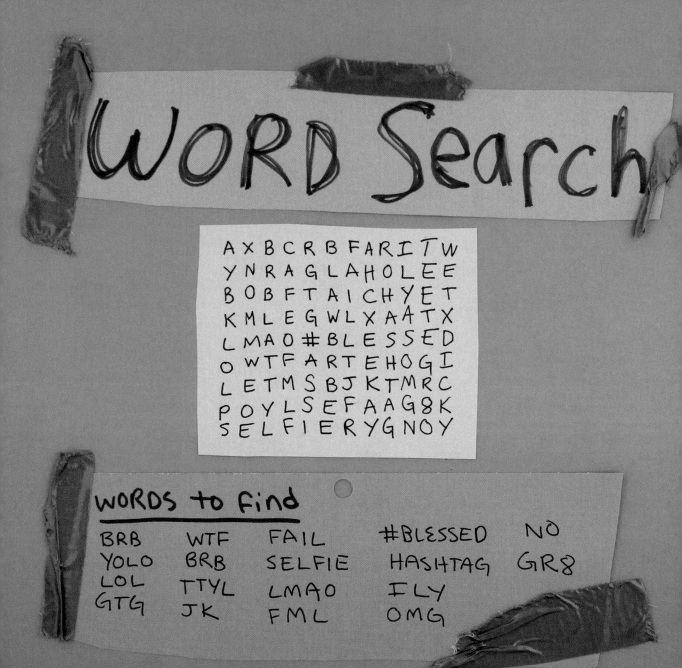

WORD Search

```
A X B C R B F A R I T W
Y N R A G L A H O L E E
B O B F T A I C H Y E T
K M L E G W L X A A T X
L M A O # B L E S S E D
O W T F A R T E H O G I
L E T M S B J K T M R C
P O Y L S E F A A G 8 K
S E L F I E R Y G N O Y
```

WORDS to find

BRB	WTF	FAIL	#BLESSED	NO
YOLO	BRB	SELFIE	HASHTAG	GR8
LOL	TTYL	LMAO	ILY	
GTG	JK	FML	OMG	

HEALTH

What is health?
Oh i'm glad you asked. Health is being healthy. like
not being sick or jumping jacks--all these kinds of
things.

Your body is a temple also it is skin and hair. So
Just saying you have to take care of it.

In this chapter i will explane the importnance of
exersize, eating rite and getting a good nights
rest.

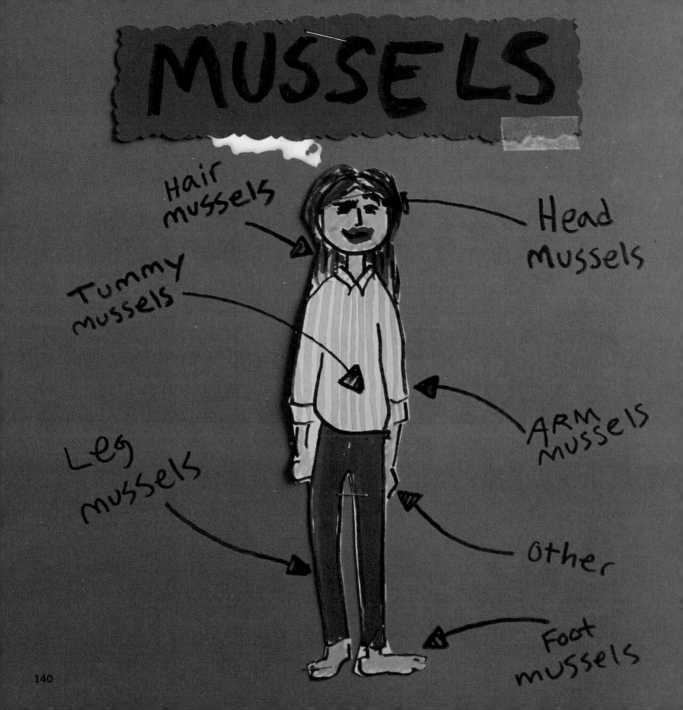

Dont PULL a MUSLe when You exersize. ALways Strench First.

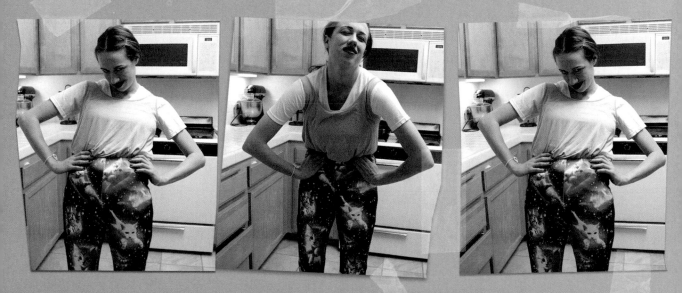

Tummy Strenches!

Down   up.   DOWN   #up.   down   UP

Face etsersize

Clikit.   Dont.   Clikit.   Dont.,

Arm exersize

Arobic exersize

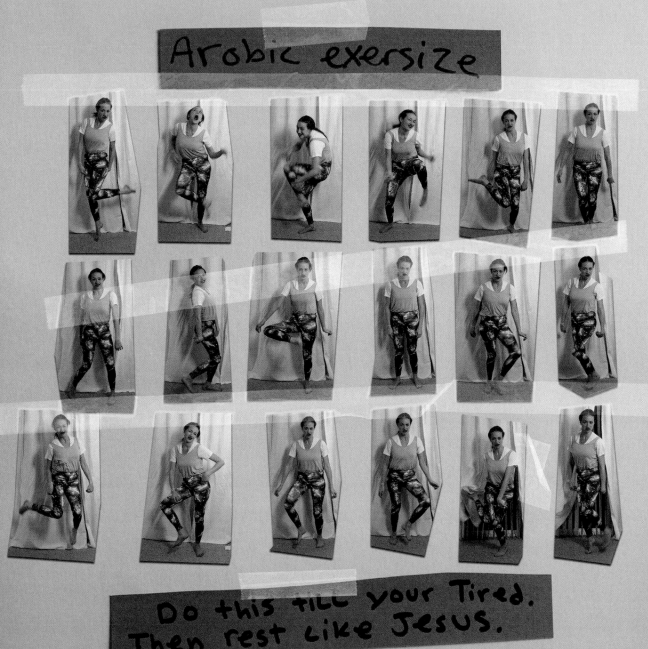

Do this till your Tired.
Then rest like Jesus.

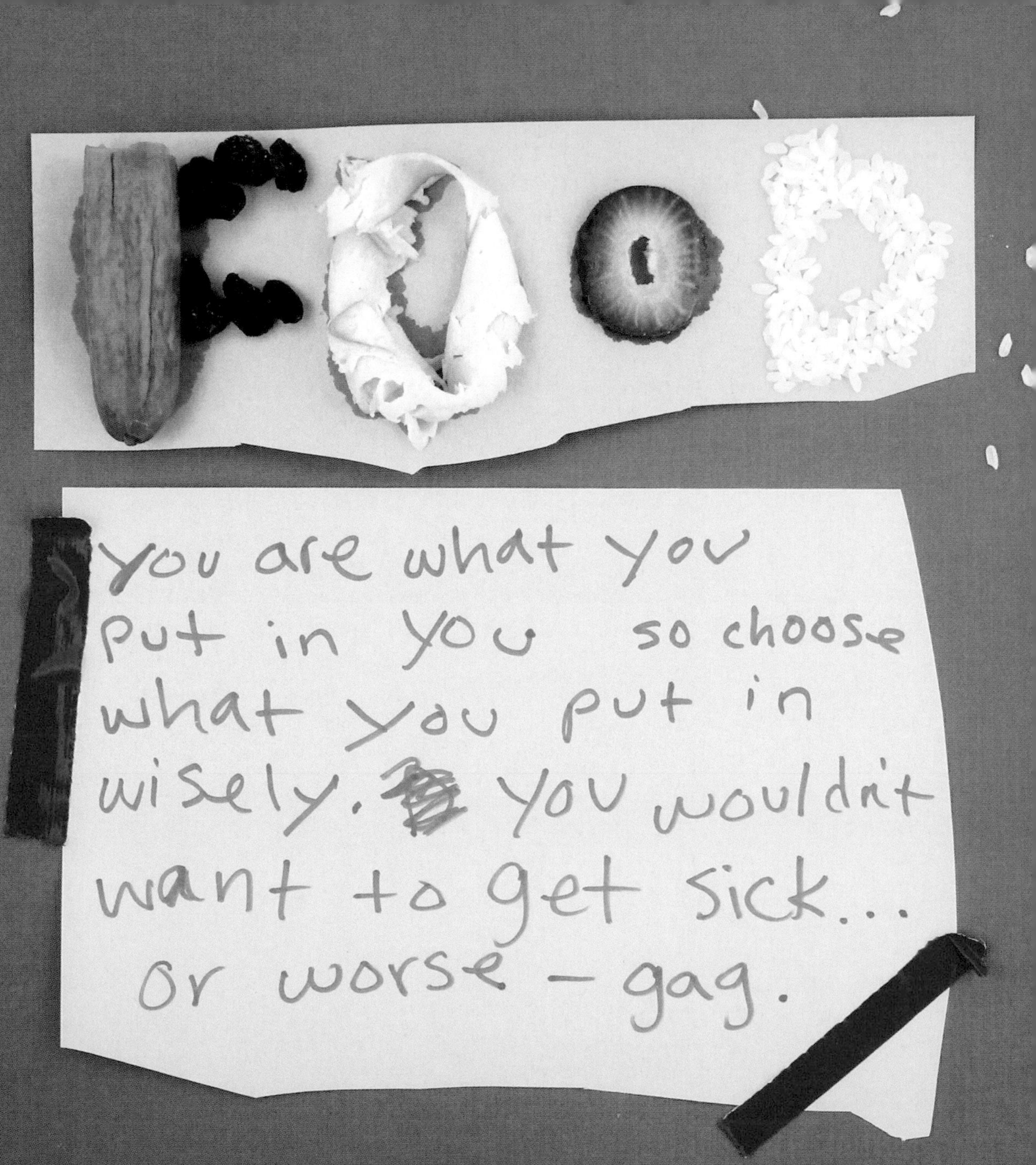

you are what you
put in you   so choose
what you put in
wisely. ~~###~~ you wouldn't
want to get sick...
or worse — gag.

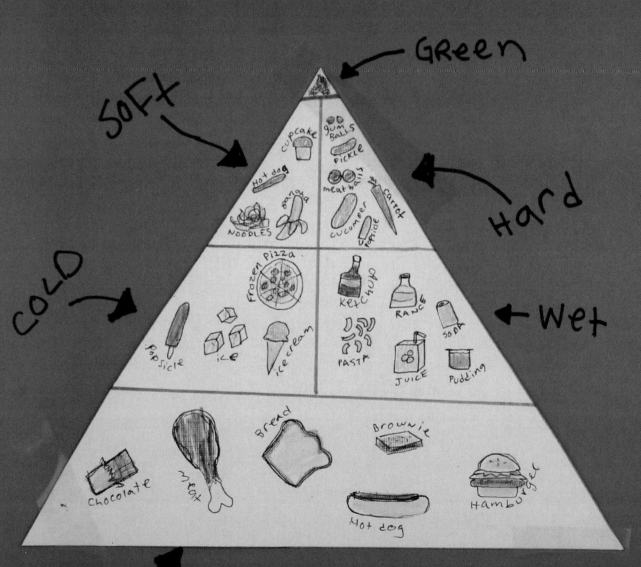

RECIPES FOR EATING

SPAGETIOS
1. Have ur uncle open the can
2. Heat it up
3. or dont
4. i like it better warmed up.
5. Put in Bowl
6. get a spoon
7. dip spoon in Bowl
8. Pick spoon up. (it will be heavier so wach out)
9. Chew it but not too much because its fun too swallow the whole "O"'s.
10. Swallow
11. Finish eating
12. Put bowl in sink
13. Find any O's that fell on the ground and eat.
14. Yell to mom

Mac n Cheese
1. make mac n cheese
2. ~~Put in Hot dogs~~
3. Eat it
4. repeet.

Couldnt find a pitchur of mac n cheese so i used this pic instead

Ambrosia

this is one of Miranda's favorite meals. Hear is my special recipe. Please try it and send me photos at Betharysings874291z@gmail.com.

INGREDIENTS

* JELLO
* CANNED FRUIT
* WHIPPED TOPPING
* RAISENS
* MARSHMALLOWS
* CORN
* MEAT (OPTIONAL)

DIRECTIONS

1. make the jello
2. add fruit, raisens, marshmallows, corn, and meat.
3. put in fridge over night and then add whipped topping.

More Recipes

HOT DOG

Microwave hot Dog

TUNA SALAD

Put BOth in Bag. squeez in mouth.

149

Dont eat greens.
Plants give us oxygin
if you eat them we
will sufficate. save
the earth. Dont eat
Plants.

Dont Eat.

Eat your ▪ Browns everyone likes good strong meets inside them. it makes you Big and helthy. Also it tastes good.

Eat it.

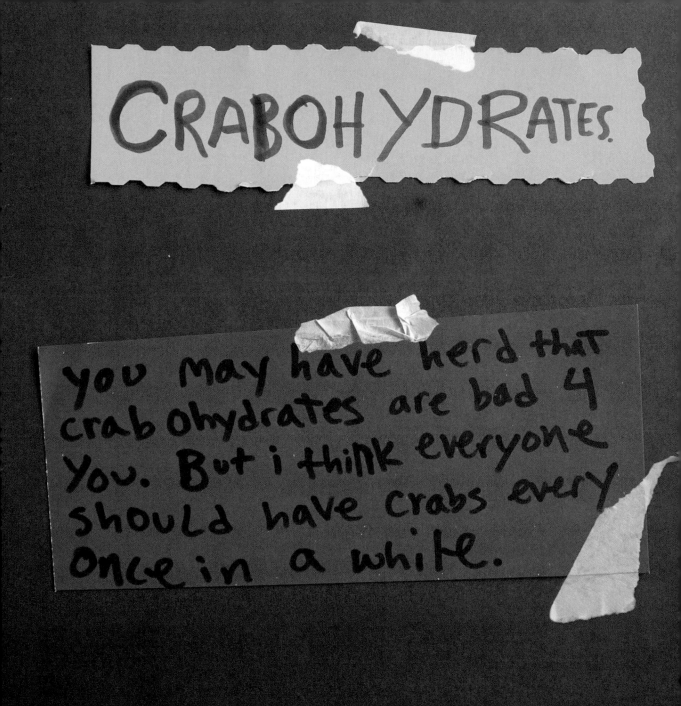

CRabs are sneaky and can look like lots of types of food.
They can be...

SOFT

CRUNCHY

ICHY

SQUINCHY

WET.

in my opinion, the more crabs you get, the better. But if your concerned about having less caRbs, you can share.

HYGENE

its important to stay
clean so you dont have
get germs. Have some
one wash you once
a week

154

WiPING

"SAVE the earth BY trapping the poo."

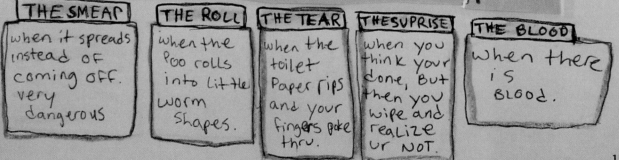

WIPE → FOLD → WIPE → FOLD → WIPE → FOLD → FOLD → WIPE → FOLD → WIPE → PUT IN POTTY

THINGS to wach out For

THE SMEAR
when it spreads
instead of
coming off.
very
dangerous

THE ROLL
when the
Poo rolls
into Little
worm
shapes.

THE TEAR
when the
toilet
Paper rips
and your
fingers poke
thru.

THE SUPRISE
when you
think your
done, But
then you
wipe and
realize
ur NOT.

THE BLOOD
when there
is
BLOOD.

How To Bath

Make Bubbles

get in all the creases

dont get hair wet

use toys

Save water by changing
water 1 a month

Dont worry about pee water.
wont change color like at
the pool

156

How to Bath Without a Bath

Hear are some ways to clean yourself w/o cleaning yourself ➤

- Kleenex
- spit
- change clothes
- perfume
- use cars smelly dangle things
- roll in fresh cut lawn
- wipe
- run thru sprinklers
- stick your head in front of fan. Let the dirt Blow off

157

How to Be Your Own Doctor.

How to Fix a Sickness

COLD	→ Blanket
Broken arm	→ Tape cast
runny Nose	→ Tampons
Throwing up	→ Stay outside
Stepped on Lego	→ No Hope
headache	→ Band aid
Something Stuck in you	→ Get help from uncle

MAKE DRUGS AT HOME!

TicTacs look like pills.

Spoonfull of pudding or soup is kind of like cough syrup.

Popsicle stick →

Puberty

CAUTION CAUTION

iF you are uNDer the age 21 PLease skip the Next 3 pages. They R inaproprite 4 you

160

PUBerty

PuBerty is a time where you get hairs and smells.

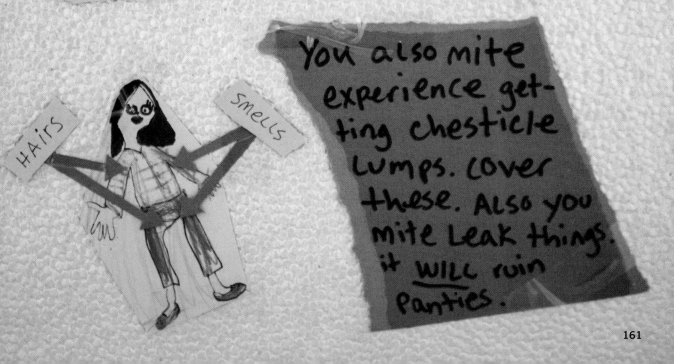

HAirs

SMELLS

You also mite experience getting chesticle lumps. cover these. ALso you mite Leak things. it WILL ruin panties.

MONTHLY LADY TIME

As a girl you sometimes get leaky after puberty and you have to clean it or you could get an infetchon or ruin panties. You can make a diaper with toilet paper or use a pad. Do NOT use tampons. They are 4 sinners. That is a exit only place!

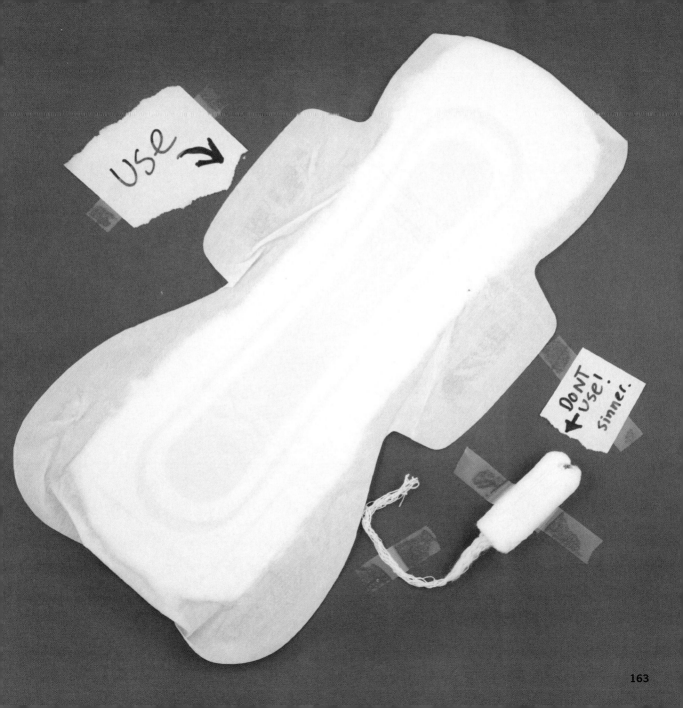

163

SLEEP

Sleep is good because when you sleep you are getting sleep and that is good. Also when you sleep you get to dream about all the things. Heare is a dream decoder so you no what your dreams mean.

DREAM DECODER

FLYING = you are gassy

FALLING = you are clumsy

DROWNING = you are thirsty

BOYS = you have wet the Bed

OPENING PRESENTS = Don't wake up. You will Be very upset.

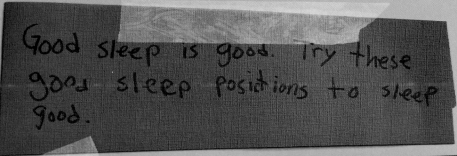

Good sleep is good. Try these good sleep positions to sleep good.

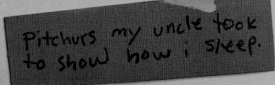

Pitchurs my uncle took to show how i sleep.

Cross word

Across
1. When you get hairs & smells
2. A way to cook something
3. Wash only 1nce a week to be...
4. Do this to Be strong
5. DeLitchous meal
6. Eat these

Down
1. These R in your arms, head & hairs
2. Staying clean
3. You should have these 1nce in a while,
4. Monthly Lady time
5. Trapping poo
6. What you should Not do with greens
7. Do this to Not pull mussels

166

Basically the Best way to have good self-esteem is to Be good at everything you do. if you are good at things with out even trying Like i am everyBody will say "oh, Your so good at it" and it will make you feel good and have good self esteem

For those of you that are Bad at things, this chapter will tech you a few lies that can trick you into having self esteem.

mirror Exercises

Look into the mirror and say these types of things.

you ARE BOOTiful.

Look how smart you are

i am a celebrity

if you are UGLY, skip to the next page.

170

171

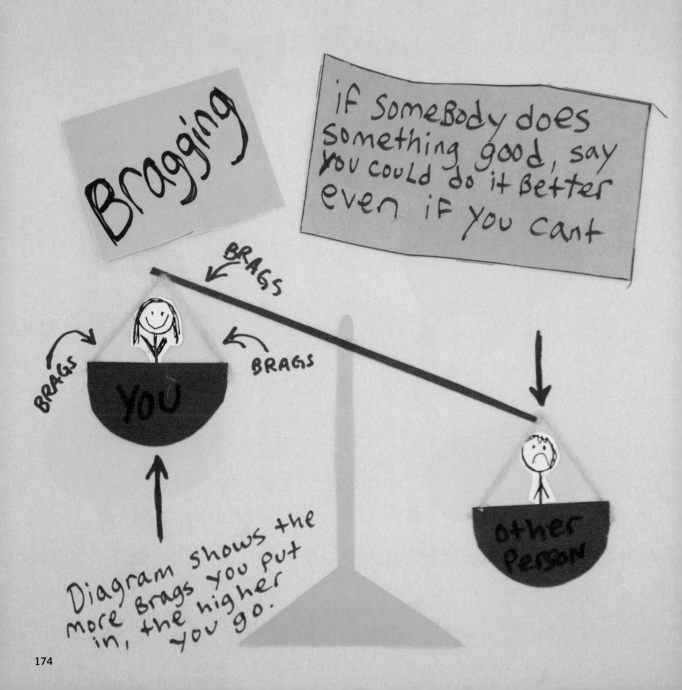

174

2 Types of Bragging

① <u>Talk about your talents:</u>
Talk about something you can do and say that you can do it the Best.

② <u>Brag over other peoples Brags:</u>
interrupt someone who is Bragging and Brag Louder and Better then them.

Games R a gr8 way to ~~their~~ higher self esteem. So play by yourself so you always win

staring contest

thumb war

Tag

Tug o' war

rock, paper
scissors

177

BODY LANGUAGE

BAD VS. GOOD

VS.

Smiling too much seems like your hiding something

Just Look Natural

VS.

VS.

Bad sitting teckneek looks weak and closed off

more available posture

VS.

Handshake is too touchy

Less germs.

178

Set RedListic expectatchons

if you have high dreams and goals, you probly wont ever achieve them and you will get depressed. So hear is a list of realistic expectatchons you should have.

- Breath
- Look
- hear
- wach TV
- eat
- potty
- sit
- read this Book
- Close your eyes
- open them
- have some juice
- go over their.
- walk
- drink the cereal milk
- Don't move
- draw a ~~star~~ dot.
- NOD
- wear clothes sometimes.

Secret code to having a happy Life. crack the code to find out what it is.

H M E A C I N D W T S V O R

Color by Number

① red
② blue
③ pink
④ brown
⑤ purple
⑥ yellow
⑦ black

1=RED 2=BLUE 3=PINK 4=BROWN 5=PURPLE
6=YELLOW 7=BLACK

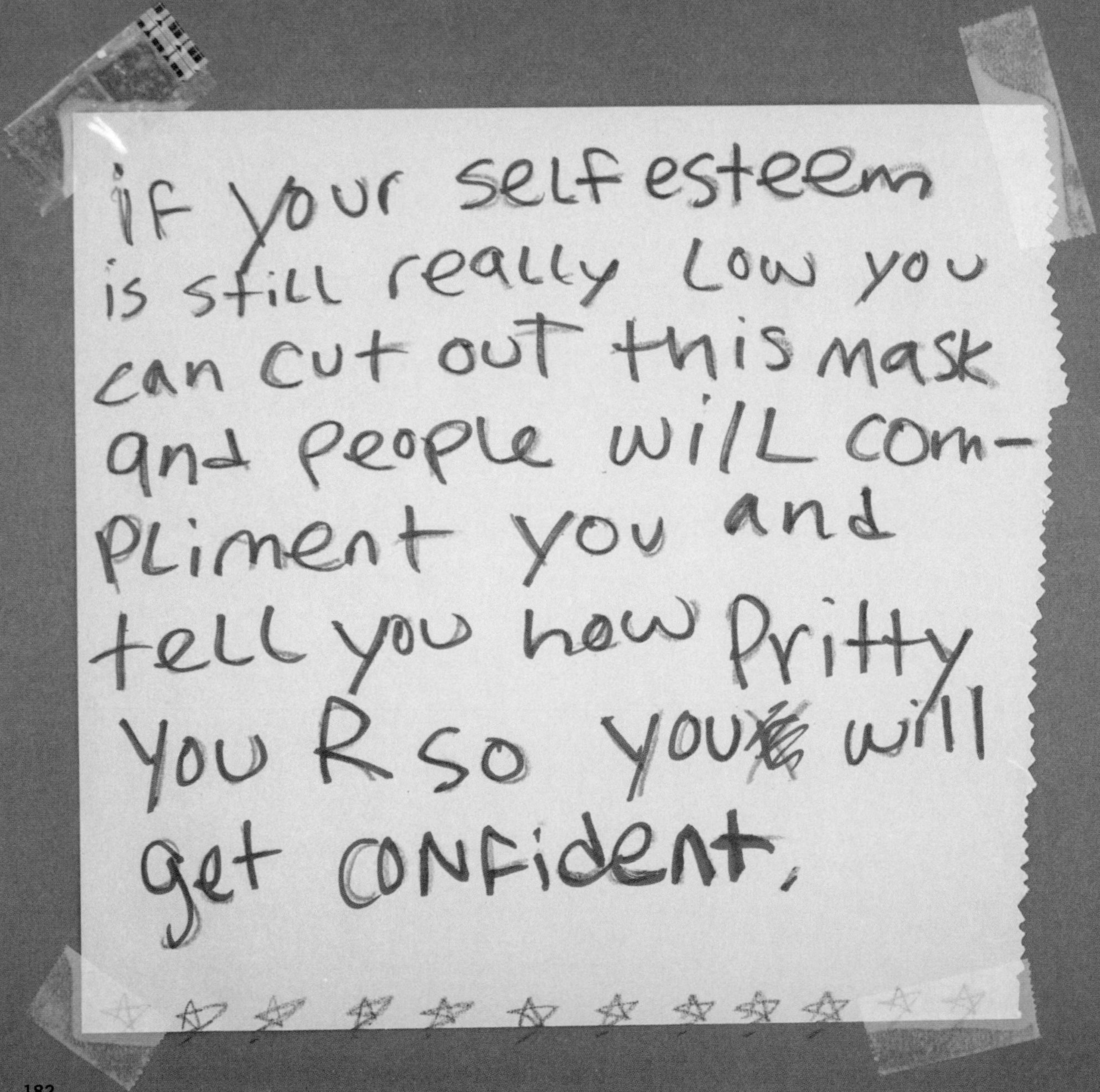

if your self esteem
is still really low you
can cut out this mask
and people will com-
pliment you and
tell you how pritty
you R so you will
get confident.

☆ ☆ ☆ ☆ ☆ ☆ ☆ ☆ ☆ ☆ ☆

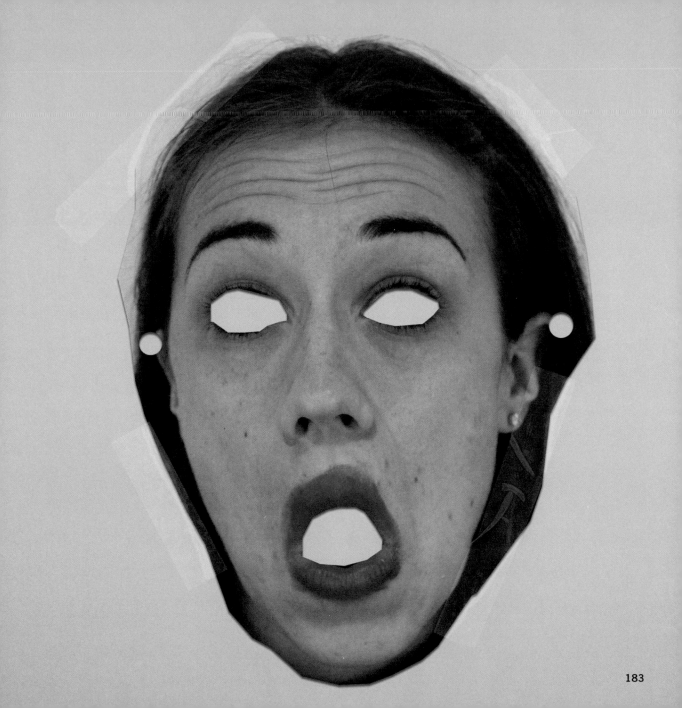

183

184

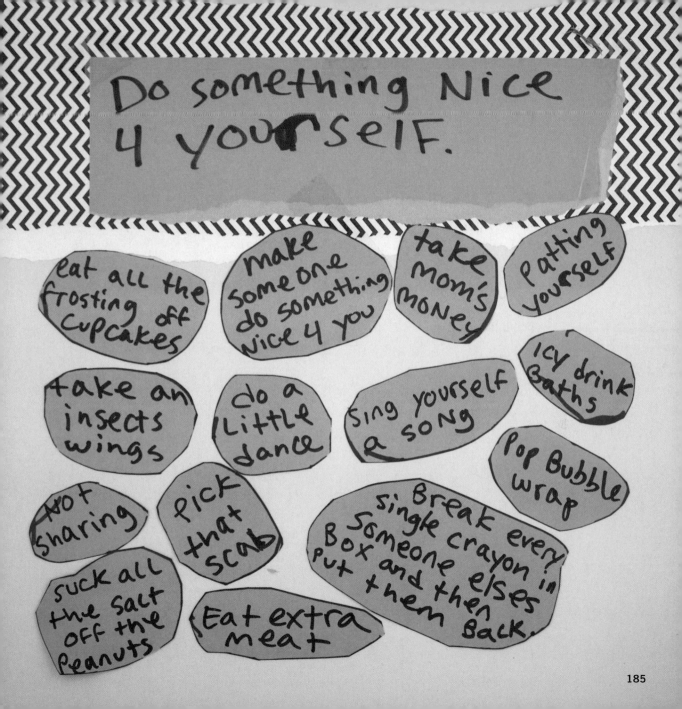

Do something Nice 4 yourself.

eat all the frosting off cupcakes

make someone do something nice 4 you

take mom's money

patting yourself

take an insects wings

do a little dance

sing yourself a song

icy drink baths

not sharing

pick that scab

pop Bubble wrap

suck all the salt off the peanuts

Eat extra meat

Break every single crayon in someone else's Box and then put them Back.

185

Self Esteem Word Scramble

FLTAHNUK ___ ___ ___ ___ (O) ___ ___ ___ ___

AYPHP (O) ___ ___ ___ ___

AiVEERCT ___ ___ ___ ___ ___ (O) ___ ___

OVLGiN ___ ___ ___ (O) ___ ___

PiGNiUVG ___ ___ ___ ___ ___ (O) ___

MREDA (O) ___ ___ ___ ___

VStiiEPO ___ ___ ___ ___ ___ ___ (O)

Final Word: ___ ___ ___ ___ ___ ___ ___

Wheather its depression or a Bad Marriage, Babies are great way to Fix things. But You cant just have a Baby! You have to make sure your Ready

Start with getting a goldfish

After 8 days when the goldfish dies, get a hamster.

After the hamster dies upgrade to a cat.

After ~~you kill the cat~~ the cat dies, get a dog

After the dog dies You are ready to have a Baby

Another good way to get ready is to practice. this is called...

BABY SITTING

Babysitting is great Because if you decide you dont like it you can just leave

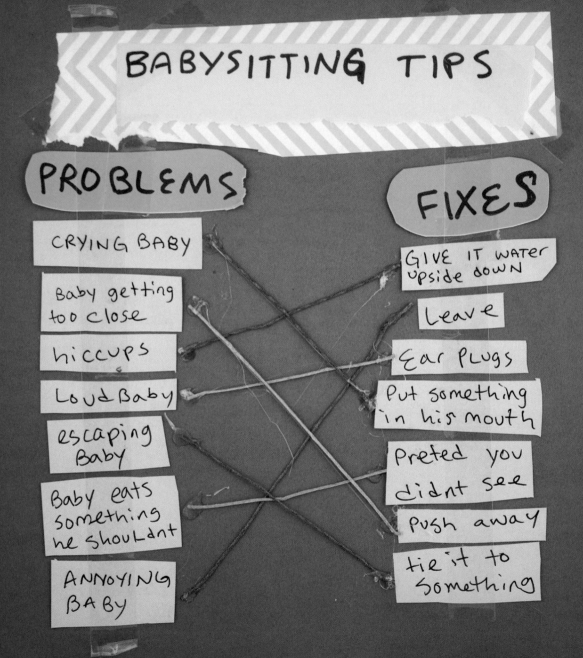

BABYSITTING TIPS

PROBLEMS

FIXES

CRYING BABY

Baby getting too close

hiccups

Loud Baby

escaping Baby

Baby eats something he shouldnt

ANNOYING BABY

GIVE IT WATER upside down

Leave

Ear Plugs

Put something in his mouth

Preted you didnt see

Push away

tie it to Something

Diaper Changing

i Dont Like using regular Diapers Because they smell too much Like Babies. A good Alternative is a towel.

STEP 1

PUT A TOWEL UNDER THE BABY's TOOKIE.

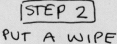

PUT A WIPE IN THERE SO You clean Less Later.

STEP3

FOLD the diaper UP and over the Baby

STEP4

TIE it all together with a rope.

191

Naps are very important Because it gives you time to do what you want. Like waching TV, eating and road trips.

192

Holding your Baby

Hear are some good positchens to Hold Your Baby with

No Hands

the Backpack

it Pooped

crusifiction

GETTING OLDER

As you have read, Babies are useless until they get older. Eventually they will Become toddlers or i like to call them: SLAVES. This is the time when you can have them do things For you.

Things a toddler can Do 4 you...

Foot massage

clean

eat crust

Fan you

Kill spiders

Fun Activities

sometimes you have to do things with kids. These few activities can be fun for you and ur children

HIDE AND SEAK

have your kid hide and then do something eslse while they are distracted

PLAYING DRESS UP

you can have them dress as a dog or a homeless

PLAY HORSEY

Looks fun right?

196

PAPER DOLL

here you **have** you're
very own **papre** doll.
dress **her** up in
different outfits for
different ocajons.

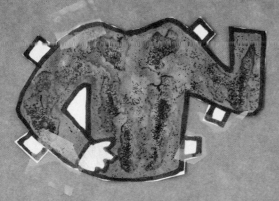
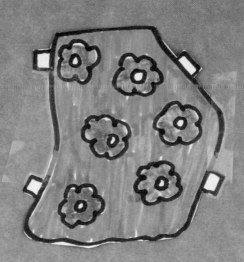

199

200

How To Play at The Playground

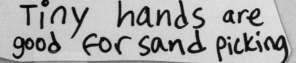

Tiny hands are good for sand picking

Kids cant Push you high enough to get scared

Kids Can catch you on the Slide

EDUCATCHON

Homeschooling is the Best option Because then you dont Have to Wake up and Drive them to school. ~~The next~~ Hear are some worksheets you can use to teach your kids

Math worksheet

1. if i had a handful of jelly beans and i ate some of them how many would be left?
   - Ⓐ some
   - Ⓑ A mouthful less than a hanful
   - Ⓒ all

2. A red train leaves Kansas at 4 o'clock a blue train leave Boston at 5. when the trains crash what color will they be?
   - Ⓐ purple
   - Ⓑ green
   - Ⓒ fire

3. How many marbles fit in this jar?
   - Ⓐ 700
   - Ⓑ 12
   - Ⓒ Yea Rite

ENGLiSH WorkSheet

FiLL iN the BLanks

1. Hair is to (AS) _____ is to
   CRUNCHY   SOFt
   (A) Hands (B) Peas (C) Loshen

2. Tickles are to (AS) _____ is to
   UNCLE   Bae
   (A) slaps (B) Kisses (C) strokes

3. spitcy is to (AS) _____ is to
   Pepper   scratchy
   (A) Rags (B) grass (C) Hair snow

4. Flaky is to (AS) Pretty is to
   SQUishy   _____
   (A) ugly (B) smart (C) BOTh

5. Hairs are to (AS) _____ are to
   Fingers   eye crusties
   (A) toes (B) sticks (C) Rags

204

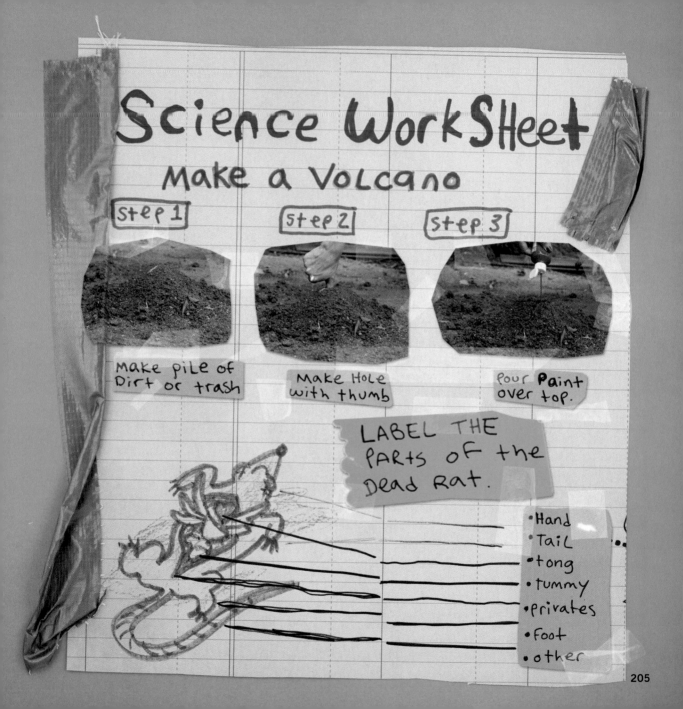

Science WorkSHeet
Make a Volcano

[step 1] [step 2] [step 3]

Make pile of
Dirt or trash

Make Hole
with thumb

Pour **Paint**
over top.

LABEL THE
PARTS OF the
Dead Rat.

- Hand
- Tail
- tong
- tummy
- privates
- foot
- other

205

Language Worksheet

Learn to say: "Hello i want some food" in **5** Different Languages...

AMERICAN
Hello i want some food

AUSTRALIAN
Gday shrimp on da Barbie

BRITISH
Pip pip tea and crumpets

MEXICAN
Hola yo Qeirro food

ITALIAN
Hia Ia wanta some-a food-a.

CANADIAN
Hello, i want some food, eh?

History Started when Christopher
Columbus Discovered America
then he had Thanksgiving with

the indians. that was the 1st
Supper. then there was
COWBOYS. then astronats.
then i was Born. Questions

↪ who started history?
what was thankgiving called?
who came Before Astronats?
who ended History?

Coloring Page

Dickshonary Meaning

Life Hacks - (lief. Hax)

Definitchon - these are do
it yourself projects that
you do at home that
make things better
and easier and
Not hard.

LIFE HACK #1

take off a Bandaid without it hurting.

THIS →

- Vaseline
- soak in water
- Time
- stick it to a carpet Before you put it on.
- Don't use one

211

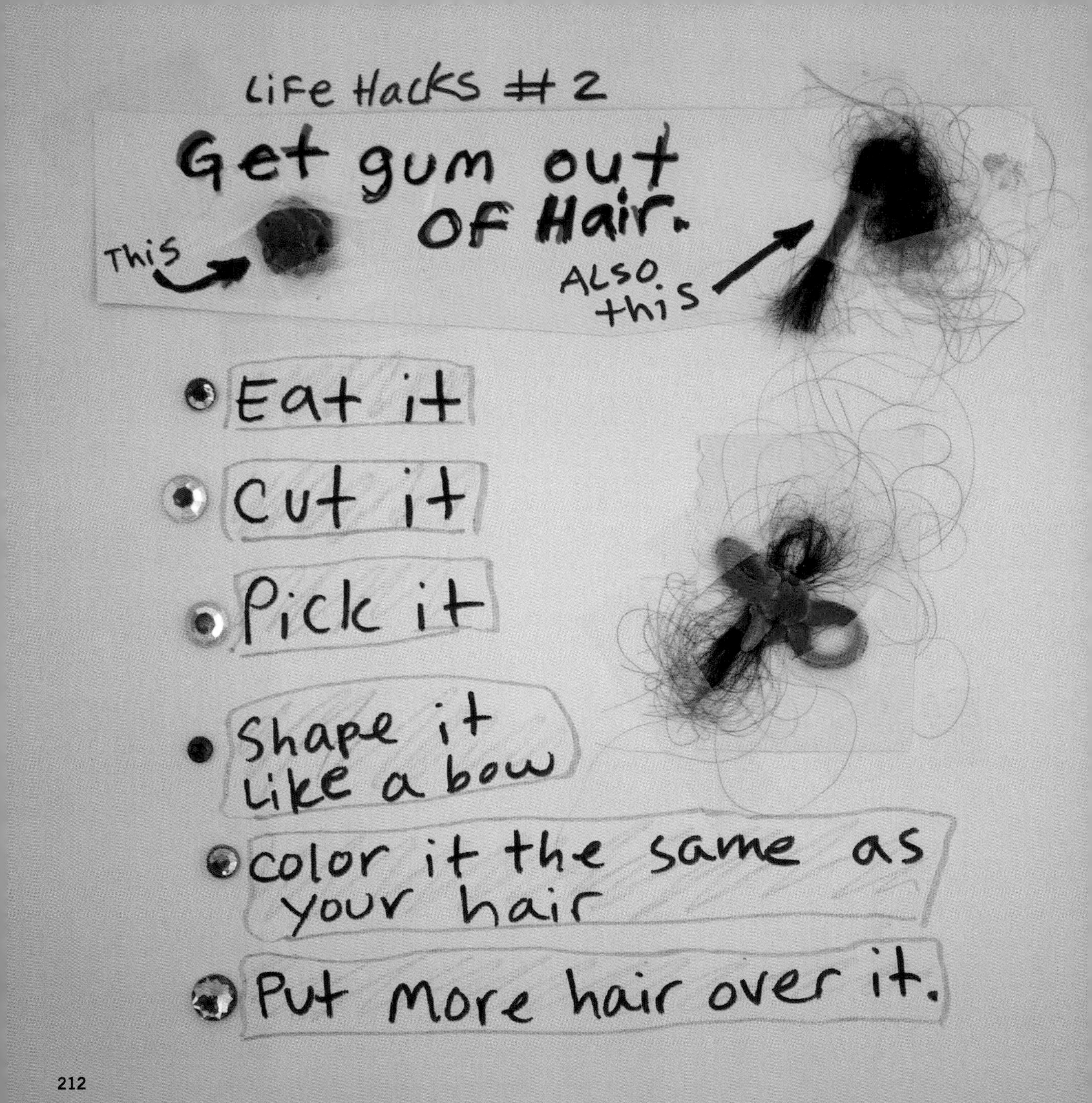

Life Hacks #2

Get gum out of Hair.

This →

ALSO. this →

- Eat it
- Cut it
- Pick it

- Shape it like a bow
- color it the same as your hair
- Put more hair over it.

212

Life Hacks #3

How To Make Homemade Shampoo

1 FIND a BOTTLE to PUT it iN.

2 use Lipgloss to Keep hair moist

3 Squirt in hand Sanitizer to keep hair clean

4 Pour in some juice to make it Smell good

5 Put it in hair to use it.

OPENING THiNGS

Hear are some things that are hard to open and how to open them.

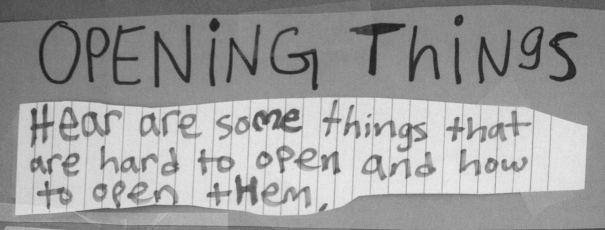

SODA CAN
cut in half with a knife.
BONUS you get two cups

Scan this with your phone to see a video tutorial.

Pickle jar
Ask your uncle to open it.
BONUS: you get to eat a pickle.

CAN OF BEANS
use a hammer.
BONUS: use Back of
hammer as a spoon

Bag of CHiPs
squeeze the Bag
BONUS: makes more
tiny chips

MUSTard Packet
Bite it
BONUS: suprise squirts

217

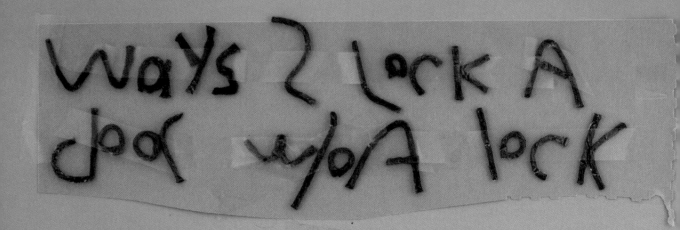

Ways 2 Lock A door w/o A lock

- Foot against the Door
- tape
- Hold it closed
- gum
- rope
- vaseline on doornob

Other uses For Household Items

Apple Pen Holder

Q-tip match

Hair & Pencil toothBrush

Sweatshirt Pants

sock hair thing

BandAid Tape

Toothpick Qtip

Phone watch

tissue Box shoe

219

How To get rid oF

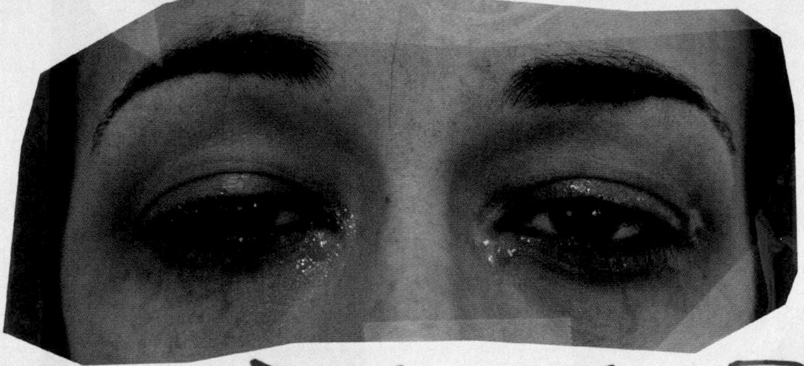

PINK EYE

STEP 1 – rub on peanut butter

STEP 2 – squeeze lemon in

STEP 3 – cover with toilet paper

STEP 4 – when it burns wipe off with piece of bread and eat it.

Get more out of your Bathroom

Stylish Hat

Toilet top cover

Toilet Rug

BiB For eating

toilet Brush

Hair Brush

toilet Paper rolls

Binoculars

Plunger

Bowl on a stick

HOW 2 FIX Pants with NO PockeTS

You will need
← This & this →

Staple Bags to Sides of Pants

Why This is Better
- Place to put hands
- you can carry things
- water proof
- you can see whats inside
- Keeps Leftovers Fresh

How to make a LAMP

① roll paper into cone

② light a candle ③ put cone over candle

223

5 things you've ben doing wrong!

① pealing a orange

pealing oranges is hard and spitcy under your nails. Dont Do it instead poke the orange and suck out the insides like a yogurt pack

WRONG

RITE

② tying your shoes

Tying your shoes is confusing and they come undone Just tape them instead

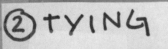

WRONG

RITE

③ sitting on the toilet

most people sit on the potty like its a chair. its not. sit on it for Best squeezing leverage

WRONG!

RITE!

④ Eating a Burrito

most People start at one end and eat there way to the other side. if you start at the middle you can suck out the guts.

WRONG!

RITE!

⑤ untangling earBuds

People spend way to much time un-tangleing headFones. just cut out the tangles and tape Back together

WRONG!

RITE!

225

DIY CRAFT iDeas

Shell Frame
get a frame and glue snails from your garden around it to make it pritty

HAiR DOLLS
twist left over or chewed up hairs into a doll shaped fun for cuddles

SCARF
use toilet paper and Decorate with markers & stickers.

PURSE
Take a paper Bag and carry it.

SNOW GLOBE
Tape a pitchur into a jar and put little white things in it like paper, skin or Finger Nails

my Friend Patrick made this Doll. Hear are the instructions

Basically you want to cut out the figure to start. You should use a sharp cutting tool like a craft knife. Cut out the main shapes and then cut out the slits that are white in the black tabs and the black lines in the main body and head sections.

I labeled everything so that the uppercase letter tab goes into the matching lowercase letter tab.

Fold the legs and connect the tabs so that they are on the inside.

Then fold the body and insert the legs into the two slits on the bottom.

Fold the sharp edges of the head and then bend down the arches of the hair. Put the body tabs into the head slits. When you do this, make sure the slits are angled up toward the back of the head or else your arms won't go in right.

Last are the arms. Fold them and pit them into the slits on the sides of the body.

You can now keep the doll by your bed, have it watch you brush your teeth or just keep it in a glass display case.

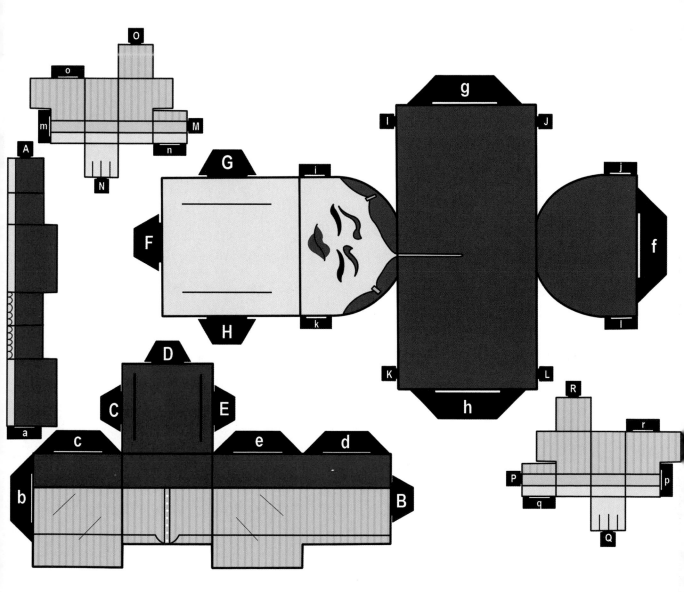

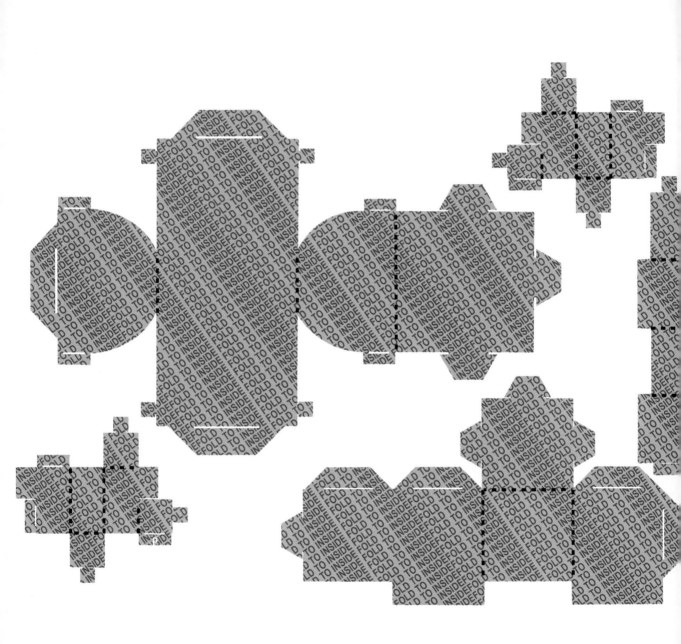

IN CONCLUTCHON

Now that you've red my book, you prabaly r better at everything now. If your not you should get an other copy of my book so you can read it again.

I want to a cours thank all my mirfandas. Also ur welcome for all of the good advice and videos and live shows that i have made for you over the years.

I promice that if you follow all of the laws in my book, you will become a better persen with your love life, your career, you're smarts and most importently your looks. Unless you arent smart or good at things.

also I'm shure that you know some horrible person that needs this book. You should get one for them as a present or tell them that they should by it for themself. That way we can change the world together.

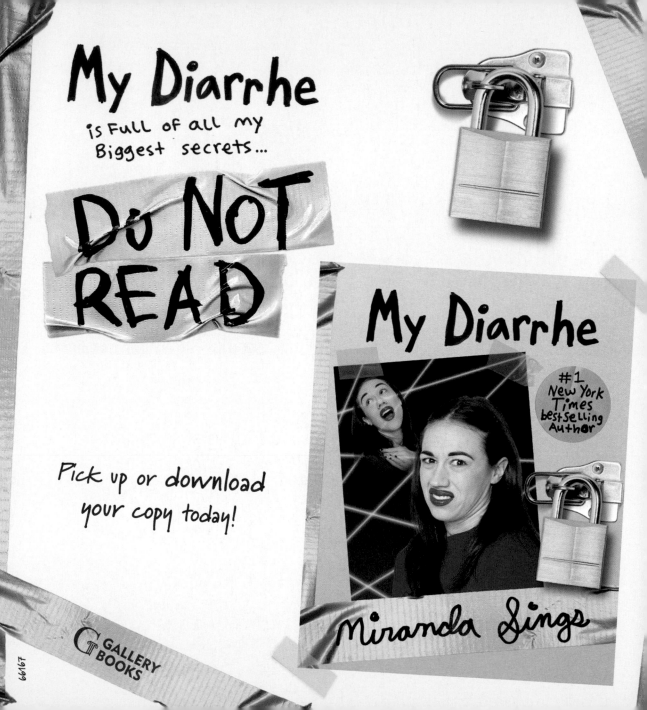